ALSO BY JULIE DE VERE HUNT

Apostle to Mary Magdalene (see page 202)

MARY
MAGDALENE'S
LEGACY

JULIE DE VERE HUNT

First published in the UK in 2019

© Julie de Vere Hunt

Marymagdaleneslegacy@gmail.com

© G2 Rights Ltd. www.g2books.co.uk

Printed and bound in Europe

ISBN: 978-1782814801

This book is dedicated to

Ratu Bagus

For you are the One who embodies today

Jesus's original uncorrupted teachings.

Om Swastiastu Ratu Bagus

ACKNOWLEDGEMENTS

To Ratu, for supporting me, my family, my writing and everything you do for everyone who crosses your path, 24 hours a day, seven days a week. Your devotion to humanity has been an inspiration to me.

To Tilda, you have walked this journey with me every step of the way - your faith, enthusiasm and encouragement kept me going when the doubt crept in!

To my publisher, Jules Gammond, for agreeing to publish my second book.

To my brother Edward for always being there for me and introducing me to Jules.

To my niece, Pippa, for proofreading the manuscript and your loving words of encouragement.

To Susanne Prabhuta who left this plane in November 2018. I thought I had finished before Christmas when you insisted I put in the Mystery School information!

To my shaking friends who have helped me promote my first book, particularly Dave in the UK and Patricia in Ireland.

To Magic Martin for keeping me well and helping to protect me during the last six months.

To Peter, my rock of ages, your actions speak louder than any words I may scribe. My daughters, princesses who shine with qualities of Mary Magdalene, and last but not least my son, who will be greater than I.

And to Mary Magdalene. You turned your back on a life of wealth and privilege to follow your heart and a life of uncertainty. I bow down to your love, trust, faith, courage, determination and patience.

You have waited a long time for your story to be heard.
Thank you for trusting me with this...

I hope I have given it justice.

CONTENTS

CONTENTS continued

INTRODUCTION

In December 1945, three Arab peasants made an astonishing archaeological discovery in Upper Egypt.

Shortly before avenging their father's murder in a blood feud, Muhammad Ali and his brothers, Ali and Abu al-Magd, were riding their camels to the Jabal al-Tarif in order to gather sabakh, a soft soil used to fertilize their crops. They hobbled their camels at the foot of the mountain, and began to dig around a massive boulder. They unexpectedly hit a red earthenware jar, almost a metre high. Muhammad Ali hesitated to break the jar, fearing the jar might contain a jinn, or spirit, that could cause trouble if released. Muhammad Ali recalled stories of hidden treasures buried in Egypt, and his love of gold overcame his fear of jinn.

He smashed the jar with his mattock, and indeed something gold in colour glinted in the bright sunlight - fragments of papyrus. When he looked excitedly into the earthenware jar, all that remained was a collection of old books - thirteen papyrus books bound in leather. These would become known as the codices of the Nag Hammadi Library, a collection of early Christian and Gnostic texts.

Muhammad Ali and his brothers returned to their home in al-Qasr, and unceremoniously dumped the books and loose papyrus leaves on the straw next to the oven. Seeing them as worthless, or even worse a bad omen, Muhammad Ali's mother burned much of the papyri in the oven.

A few weeks later, Muhammad Ali and his brothers avenged their father's death by murdering Ahmad Isma'il. Their mother had warned the brothers to keep their mattocks sharp, which they put to good use by hacking off their father's enemy's limbs, ripped out his heart and devoured it amongst them. This for them was the final act of revenge. But not final for the son of Ahmad Isma'il, the butchered man. Shortly after, he shot up the funeral cortege of Muhammad Ali's family, wounding Muhammad Ali and killing a number of his clan.

Fearing that the police investigating the murder of Ahmed Ismail would search his house and discover the books, Muhammad Ali asked the priest, al-Qummus Basiliyus Abd al-Masih, to keep some of the books for him.

Whilst the brothers were being interrogated for murder, Raghib, a local history teacher, saw one of the books and suspected it had value. He sent it to a friend in Cairo to find out its worth.

Sold on the black market through antiquities dealers in Cairo, the manuscripts soon attracted the attention of Egyptian Government Officials. They bought one, and confiscated ten and a half of the thirteen leather-bound books (codices), and deposited them in the Coptic Museum in Cairo. A large part of the thirteenth codex was smuggled out of Egypt and offered for sale in America. Professor Gilles Quispel from Utrecht University in Holland heard about the codex and urged the Jung Foundation in Zurich to buy it. This he succeeded in doing, but was dismayed to find that some of the pages were missing. He flew to Cairo in the spring of 1955 and went to the Coptic Museum to borrow photographs of the missing pages.

"These are the secret words which the living Jesus spoke, and which the twin, Judas Thomas, wrote down."

Quispel had in his hands the opening lines of the Greek Gospel of Thomas - just one of the fifty-two texts discovered at Nag Hammadi. The Gospel of Thomas is not a narrative like the New Testament gospels, rather a list of sayings attributed to Jesus. Sayings in Thomas are strikingly similar to sayings from Matthew and Luke; such as parables about the kingdom of God, including the parable of the mustard seed and the parable of the sower, and sayings such as "Blessed are the poor, for yours is heaven's kingdom". Some scholars believe the Gospel of Thomas is an early collection of Jesus's teaching - possibly one that Matthew and Luke used to compose their own gospels?

What Muhammad Ali discovered at Nag Hammadi were Coptic translations made about 1,500 years ago of still more ancient manuscripts. The originals themselves had been in Greek, the language of the New Testament. Examination of the datable papyrus used to thicken the leather bindings, and of the Coptic script, places them AD 350-400. However, scholars have failed to agree on the dating of the original texts, with some proposing the second half of the first century, even earlier than Mark, Matthew, Luke and John.

So why were these texts buried? The Nag Hammadi texts, and others like them, were denounced as heresy by orthodox Christians in the middle of the second century. The campaign against heresy involved an admission of its persuasive power - but the church prevailed. By the time of Emperor Constantine's conversion, when Christianity became an officially approved religion in the fourth century, Christian bishops now commanded the police. Possession of books denounced as heretical was made a criminal offence. Copies of such books were burned and destroyed.

These diverse texts range from secret gospels, poems and quasi-philosophical descriptions of the origin of the universe, to myths, magic and instructions for mystical practice.

Most of the writings use Christian terminology related to a Jewish heritage. These Christians are now called gnostics. From the Greek word gnosis, it means 'insight', an intuitive process of knowing oneself. And to know oneself, is to know human nature and human destiny.

All religious traditions acknowledge the world is imperfect. Few, if any, are able to account for all the suffering and pain that exists in our world. The Gnostics have come up with their own reasoning; the world is flawed because it was created in a flawed manner. Gnostics believe there is a true, ultimate and transcendent God, who is beyond all created universes and who never created anything. He (or it) emanated from within Himself the substance of all there is in all the worlds, visible and invisible. So, all is part of God, but many portions of the original divine essence have been projected so far from their original source they have undergone corrupt changes. The basic Gnostic myth refers to Aeons, intermediate deific beings who exist between the ultimate True God and ourselves. They, together with the True God, comprise the realm of Fullness (Pleroma) where divinity exists fully. In contrast, we are in an existential state, sometimes called emptiness.

Sophia ("Wisdom") is one of the aeonial beings who, from her own being, proceeded to emanate a flawed consciousness; that is, a being named Demiurgos or 'half-maker'. Demiurgos imagined himself to be the ultimate and absolute God, who became the creator of the material and psychic cosmos. There is a true deific component within creation, but it is not recognized by Demiurgos and his cosmic minions, the Archons or rulers.

Human nature mirrors the duality found in the world; in part it was made by the false creator God, Demiurgos, and in part it consists of the light of the True God. Humans, therefore, contain a perishable physical component as well as a spiritual component, which is a fragment of the divine essence, referred to as the divine spark.

Human beings are often unaware of this divine spark within them. The Demiurgos and his Archons are intent upon keeping men and women ignorant of their true nature and destiny. All our earthly attachments keep us enslaved to these lower cosmic rulers. Death releases the divine spark, but unless the individual has attained gnosis (salvation through knowledge of spiritual mysteries) prior to death, they will inevitably reincarnate back into the physical world. Fortunately, from earliest times Messengers of the Light have come from the True God to assist us in our quest for gnosis. A few of these are mentioned in Gnostic texts; Seth (the third Son of Adam), Jesus and the prophet Mani. Most Gnostics regard Jesus as the principal saviour figure.

Most Gnostic texts take the form of myths: this does not mean that they are stories that are untrue, but that the truths embodied in these myths are of a different order from the dogma of theology or statements of philosophy. Many of the texts refer to Old Testament scriptures, the letters of Paul and the New Testament gospels. They include the same characters; Jesus and his disciples, but there are striking differences.

In the Gnostic texts Jesus speaks of illusion and enlightenment, not of sin and repentance like the Jesus of the New Testament. Instead of redeeming us from our sins, he comes as a guide who facilitates spiritual understanding. When the disciple attains enlightenment, Jesus is no longer their spiritual master - they have become equal.

To the Gnostic, commandments and rules are not necessary for salvation. Salvation is only achieved by gnosis. Rules may be useful in structuring a peaceful and ordered society, and for maintaining harmonious relations within social groups. Gnostics resist 'ethics' and 'morality' being imposed upon them, seeing them as covert systems originating from the demiurge, Demiurgos, and designed to serve his purposes, not ours.

Gnosticism encourages non-attachment and non-conformity to the world, a 'being in the world, but not of it'; a lack of egotism, and a respect for the freedom and dignity of other beings. In the fullness of time, with earnest striving for gnosis, every spiritual being will be reunited with its Higher Self and be able to enter the Pleroma.

By AD 200 Christianity had become an institution headed by bishops, priests and deacons, who considered themselves guardians of the only 'true faith'. All other viewpoints were rejected as heresy. No wonder they wanted to 'stamp out' the gnostic movement, which offered a powerful and enticing alternative to the church institution!

Although the gnostic gospels are assigned to the apostles, scholars are unable to agree on who actually wrote them. It is not unreasonable to assume they were written in Egypt as there are frequent references to Egypt in the earlier ones and the Nag Hammadi codices were found there. The Nag Hammadi codices have been beset from beginning to end by a persistent curse of political roadblocks, litigations and scholarly rivalries which meant a first translated edition was not published until 1975.

Among the priceless treasures in the Nag Hammadi library is the Gospel of Mary. Dr. Karen King, Professor of Divinity at Harvard Divinity School, believes it was written during the time of Jesus. She defends the position of Mary Magdalene as the author as she was the only figure who could have written from the perspective of a close disciple, a witness to the ministry of Jesus, as someone who experienced a vision of the glorified Jesus, and someone in contest with Peter. These gospels emphasise the role of Mary Magdalene and suggest that a focus on the idea of a virgin birth and bodily resurrection miss the real point of Jesus' teachings.

The papyri were finally given to the Coptic Museum in Cairo in 1975. Eleven complete books and fragments of two others are preserved there, amounting to well over a thousand pages of the 1945 discovery.

Marvin Meyer's book 'The Nag Hammadi Scriptures ' provides a translation with commentary which I highly recommend, but as I doubt many of you will plough your way through 1,000 pages (neither have I), I have taken the liberty of choosing extracts from the codices. They are also available to read online for free at www.gnosis.org.

Personally, when I first started reading the texts I had a hard time getting my head around some of them, The Secret Book of John in particular. As I persisted, layers of resistance fell away as I became accustomed to the way they were written. They were written in allegorical and mythical form to deliver a deeper, underlying meaning. A myth is not only a story, it is a statement made in symbols. The language of the unconscious is symbolic. A symbol speaks directly to the soul, and is understood by the soul, even when consciousness does not understand. When a symbol touches the soul there is a change. Every myth takes its origin in human inspiration. Inspiration (from the Latin inspirare) means a message from the spirit, the breath of life. The spirit speaks from the macrocosmos and gives us answers to the unanswered. Meeting this spirit fulfils a destiny way beyond our material world and these texts are trying to show us the way.

There is a long standing tradition that Jesus only imparted advanced teachings to the spiritual elite while withholding them from the uninitiated.

Jesus said, *"I disclose my mysteries to those who are worthy of my mysteries."* Gospel of Thomas.

This led to a split in the early Christian church: the Church of St Peter (the Roman Catholic Church or the Petrine Church), which spread the universal teachings of Jesus; and a clandestine Christian church (sometimes called the Johannine Church) whose members were privy to Jesus' secret teachings largely influenced by the writings in The Secret Book of John.

In the middle of all this reading and research, I came across a book called The Bible Code written by Michael Drosnin in 1997. Sir Isaac Newton was convinced there was a hidden code in the Bible that might reveal the future. He learned Hebrew and spent decades trying to find it. With the advent of computers, an Israeli mathematician called Professor Eliyahu Rips broke the code which foretells events that happened thousands of years after the Bible was written. It foresaw World War II, the Moon landing, and both Kennedy assassinations to name but a few.

According to Professor Rips, the whole Bible Code had to be written at once. The history of the human race recorded more than 3000 years ahead of time. Professor Rips is more cautious about using the code to foresee the future. He sees the code like a hologram, where each part contains within it the information that codes for the whole (see 'Apostle to Mary Magdalene: Z is for Zero Point Field). The universe is also a hologram. And so we return to quantum physics...

Professor Rips thinks we have only scratched the surface; within the code lie a myriad of potential outcomes, not predetermined, but influenced by you and me. In other words we are creating our own reality. And we are not alone. Professor Rips said;

"This is the product of a higher intelligence. It may want us to understand, but it may not want us to understand. The code may not reveal the future to us unless we are worthy."

My cellular memory has revealed that some of the gnostic gospels are also coded, including The Secret Book of John. I have highlighted the ones I believe are coded in bold in the list of Nag Hammadi codices on the following pages.

I believe that we are worthy, and now is the time..

PROLOGUE

"This is the book Great Seth (son of Adam) composed and placed high in the mountains on which the sun has not risen and cannot rise... Great Seth placed it on the mountain called Cheraxio, so that, at the end of times and ages, it may come forth and appear to this holy incorruptible generation of the Great Saviour and those dwelling with them in love... Amen" The Gospel of the Egyptians

APRIL 367 CE: NAG HAMMADI

Athanasius, the orthodox patriarch of Alexandria, wrote an Easter letter to all the monasteries in Egypt. The letter listed those books that were to be considered 'acceptable' and included in the Bible - the oldest known list of the 27 books in the New Testament. All other writings were considered heretical and were to be destroyed at once. Unsurprisingly, the Nag Hammadi codices were not on this list.

And so it was time...

The monks were prepared. The word was given and two of the younger brothers, Abu and Kahlil, prepared for their mission that night. There was no time to be wasted. Fortunately, it was almost full moon and they would not need lamps to light their way and alert their enemies. Kahlil, slight in stature, carefully packed the collection of books in his old battered leather satchel. Safely inside his satchel were the 13 papyrus codices and two diaries. The diaries of Mary Magdalene and her daughter Sarah, chronicling what happened after the Darkest Day when Yeshua was crucified.

Abu, an ox of a man, effortlessly lifted the large earthenware jar to the saddle of his camel and bound it in place. Abu nodded at Kahlil and they rode into the night towards Jabal al Tarif. Abu led the way and after a few hours, stopped, looked around to ensure there was no one around, dismounted and hobbled the camels.

Abu carefully unloaded the large jar onto his shoulder and Kahlil carried the satchel and two spades they would need to dig a hole and bury their treasure. Khalil, nimble and light on his feet like a mountain goat, led the way, following an undefined but pre-agreed route. Abu, slowed down by his load, followed at a steady pace. After climbing steeply for half an hour or so, Kahlil stopped by a huge boulder, laid down his satchel and started digging in the soft soil against the cliff face. Abu arrived and joined in with the digging - with two of them progress was swift. The hole had to be at least six feet deep to completely cover the jar and its precious contents.

Whilst Kahlil placed the books inside the jar, Abu set about making a seal out of sand and water. The sand contained lime and when mixed with water formed a quick-drying mortar which would make an airtight seal. He used a palette knife to apply the mortar to the rim of the jar and then placed a bowl on top, held in place by a large rock for good measure. Between them they lowered the jar into the hole and put the soil back, burying the jar well below the surface. They smoothed the surrounding soil with the soles of their sandals so it looked undisturbed.

An owl swooped past and startled them - they smiled at one another in relief. But no-one came this way, and they were sure they hadn't been followed.

It was done.

"But thou, O Daniel, shut up the words and seal the book until the time of the End." Old Testament, Daniel 12:4

LIST OF NAG HAMMADI CODICES

CODEX I (also known as the Jung Codex)

The Prayer of the Apostle Paul
The Secret Book of James
The Gospel of Truth
The Treatise on the Resurrection
The Tripartite Tractate

CODEX II

The Secret Book of John
The Gospel of Thomas
The Gospel of Philip
The Hypostasis of the Archons
On the Origin of the World
The Exegesis of the Soul
The Book of Thomas the Contender

CODEX III

The Secret Book of John
Holy Book of the Great Invisible Spirit (The Gospel of the Egyptians)
Eugnostos the Blessed
The Sophia of Jesus Christ
The Dialogue of the Saviour

CODEX IV

The Secret Book of John
Holy Book of the Great Invisible Spirit (The Gospel of the Egyptians)

CODEX V

Eugnostos the Blessed
The Revelation of Paul
The First Revelation of James
The Second Revelation of James
The Revelation of Adam
The Gospel of Judas

CODEX VI

The Acts of Peter and the Twelve Apostles
The Thunder, Perfect Mind
Authoritative Teaching
The Concept of our Great Power
Republic Plato (heavily modified with gnostic concepts)
The Discourse on the Eighth and Ninth - a Hermetic treatise
The Prayer of Thanksgiving - a Hermetic prayer
Asclepius 21-29 - another Hermetic treatise

CODEX VII

The Paraphrase of Shem
The Second Treatise of the Great Seth
Gnostic Apocalypse of Peter
The Teachings of Silvanus
The Three Steles of Seth

CODEX VIII

Zostrianos
The Letter of Peter to Philip

CODEX IX

Melchizedek
The Thought of Norea
The Testimony of truth

CODEX X

Marsanes

CODEX XI

The Interpretation of Knowledge
A Valentinian Exposition, On the Anointing, On Baptism and
On the Eucharist

Allogenes
Hypsiphrone

CODEX XII

The Sentences of Sextus
The Gospel of Truth
Fragments

CODEX XIII

Trimorphic Protennoia
On the Origin of the World

Those texts highlighted in bold are coded

PART I: MARY'S DIARY

CODEX II: THE GOSPEL OF PHILIP

Three Women Named Mary

Three women always walked with the Master: Mary his mother, her sister, and Mary of Magdala, who is called his companion...

Wisdom and Mary of Magdala

The companion of the Saviour is Mary of Magdala. The Saviour loved her more than all the disciples and he kissed her often on her mouth.

The other disciples said to him, "Why do you love her more than all of us?"

The Saviour answered and said to them,

"Why don't I love you like her? If a blind person and one who can see are both in darkness, they are the same. When the light comes, who can see will see the light, and the blind person will stay in darkness."

CHAPTER I

April 33 CE: Bethany

I was well born, descended of royal stock. My father's name was Syrus and my mother Eucharus. Sadly, my mother died when I was nine and my father when I was sixteen. And so with my brother Lazarus and sister Martha we owned Magdalum, a walled town two miles from Genezareth, along with Bethany, not far from Jerusalem, and a considerable part of Jerusalem itself. We divided the holdings amongst ourselves so that I owned Magdalum (hence my name Magdalene), Lazarus kept the property in Jerusalem and Bethany was Martha's. It was an unsettled time in my life and I gave myself to the pleasures of the flesh, Lazarus to the military, and Martha kept close watch over our estates and took care of the needs of her armed men, her servants and the poor.

So I was very rich, and sensuous pleasure often keeps company with great wealth. I was renowned for my beauty, my wealth and the way I gave my body to pleasure - so much so I was commonly known as "the sinner".

Meanwhile, Jesus, also known as Yeshua, was preaching here and there, and guided by divine will, I hastened to the house of Simon the leper, where I had heard he was preaching over dinner. He looked at me with his liquid sapphire blue eyes - a colour and iridescence I had never seen before - lively, yet still, a deep well of mystery. He seemed from another world... His face overflowed with compassion and non-judgement, and to my embarrassment I found myself weeping. Being a sinner I did not dare mingle with the righteous, but stayed back and washed the Lord's feet with my tears, dried them with my hair, and anointed them with precious ointment.

Simon the Pharisee thought to himself that if this man were a true prophet, he would never allow a sinful woman to touch him, but Yeshua rebuked him and told me all my sins were forgiven. He cast seven demons out of me and set me on fire with love for him. He defended me when the Pharisee said I was unclean, when Martha said I was lazy, when Judas called me wasteful. Seeing me weep he could not contain his own tears. For love of me he raised my brother who had been dead for four days, and he freed Martha from the blood flux she had suffered from for seven years.

And then I remembered. He was the One. The One I had learned about when I attended the Mystery School in Alexandria some six years earlier when I was twenty years old. The ancients had foretold centuries ago that someone would be brought in with a very high consciousness, start as a normal human, and transform himself to an immortal state through resurrection. But he needed help. And I was told by my teachers that I would be part of the divine plan..

And so from that day forth I followed him, and he showered me with so many marks of his love for me. He sought my counsel and he defended me at all times. We were very different and yet complimentary; Yeshua was more of the water and air elements, whereas I lean towards fire and earth. But above all he was my twin soul - I will never forget the first time we became as one, so exquisite and quite unlike anything I had experienced before..

Joseph of Arimathea said it was not safe for me to remain in Jerusalem - there was no accounting for what the Romans might do to quell the unrest in Jerusalem after the 'Darkest Day' when my beloved was crucified.

In his dying hours Yeshua had made Joseph promise to look after me - I was with child and Yeshua wanted to be sure me and my precious cargo would be safe... It should have been Peter as leader of the apostles, but he and the others were nowhere to be seen, fearing for their safety.

Joseph had begged the authorities to release Yeshua's body to him; his love for Yeshua overcame his fear for his own safety. It was Joseph's tomb Yeshua was laid to rest in, fulfilling the prophecy in Isaiah Chapter 53;

"He was assigned a grave with the wicked, and with the rich in his death, though he had done no violence, nor was any deceit in his mouth".

At least I saw him! I will be eternally grateful that I actually saw him outside the tomb on the third day, happy and smiling, with no wounds, in a clean, white robe. Although I knew it was part of the plan, the memory of him hanging on the cross still haunts me while I sleep at night - at least I know now he is safe from those who want to harm him, with his Father in the Kingdom of Heaven.

I was reluctant to leave Yeshua but he urged me to tell the other Apostles and I sped to find them. They were hiding in Levi's family home in Jerusalem...But Andrew and Peter did not like what I had to say and disbelieved me... I was upset. Peter was always jealous of me, because of my relationship with Yeshua. Levi defended me. Yeshua would have done if he had still been alive, but I was on my own now.

I left them and made my way home to Bethany to join Lazarus and Martha. Joseph, the two Marys, the Virgin Mary and Mary Salome, were also there. Joseph said we would leave at first light on foot for Joppa, some 30 miles to the west on the Mediterranean coast. We would then sail 260 miles or so by boat to Alexandria, on the northern coast of Egypt.

Joseph was a wealthy tin merchant; he was Minister of Mines, appointed by Emperor Augustus, and had contacts in Alexandria. He said Alexandria was the nearest safe haven; it was a big bustling city with a sizeable Jewish population who were not only tolerated, but respected by the Roman authorities.. They lived side by side with the Greeks and Egyptians; the Romans allowed them autonomy, even their own council, which was unusual to say the least. Joseph said he would be able to secure lodgings for us in Delta, the Jewish quarter of Alexandria, with one of his business contacts.

Of course I knew Alexandria well. Before she was married my mother had trained as a priestess at the Great Mother Isis Temple School in Alexandria, and even though she died when I was young she had already encouraged me to follow in her path. She wore a golden serpent on her left arm, spiralling up from the elbow, signifying she was an initiate of this Temple School. The serpent represents the Kundalini energy at the base of the spine, which when activated through specific energetic or Tantric practices, can spiral up and shift consciousness in an individual beyond the mind into Cosmic Awareness. This symbol of resurrection indicates the wearer has been initiated into the mysteries of Isis, and serves the Great Mother's creation and its awakening from 'spiritual death' or separation consciousness. The electro (male)-magnetic (female) energy of the earth also flows in a serpentine fashion, called ley lines. These ley lines circumnavigate the earth to form a consciousness grid. The seven ancient wonders of the world are located on ley lines and are energetic 'power points'. This energy can be channelled and directed for the benefit of the earth and all its life forms.

Alexandria was an international multi-ethnic centre of learning. I had money and could afford to go there. In contrast to Judea, women had obtained a more advanced state of emancipation socially, politically and legally. Women were admitted to Temple Schools alongside men, particularly that of the Isis Temple School. Some of the initiations were challenging, but the blessings were countless. I specialized in healing and blessing work. This is where I learned about the Mystery School of Akhenaten, the Law of One. I was fortunate to find it, and even more blessed to be admitted after graduating from the Isis Temple School. Admittance was by invitation only, and only a few from our class were granted that honour. Its symbol is the Right Eye of Horus, representing protection, usually with a blue iris;

Right Eye of Horus

It being a mystery school, I was sworn to secrecy and we all took oaths. Mystery schools had been set up over the ages by small groups of people to break up the power circles that had been created by the wealthy and all powerful priests who controlled the people. The aim of these schools was to protect advanced scientific information encoded in texts, drawings and art that would appear ordinary if they fell into the wrong hands. Some schools did not write anything down - the information was passed down orally as pure sound syllables and ultrasonic frequencies.

Akhenaten was an ancient pharaoh of Egypt and ruled for just seventeen years from 1351-1334 BC. Akhenaten challenged polytheism; at that time the people worshipped many gods and their religious beliefs were controlled by the priesthood. Akhenaten took a brave stance and told the people there was only one God, and more importantly they could access God from inside themselves. The priests were outraged as they were effectively made redundant overnight. Egypt had one of the strongest military armies in the world at this time, but Akhenaten was a pacifist and refused to conquer other lands, so he was unpopular with the military as well! Akhenaten's consciousness was very high and his aim was to teach immortality to his followers - during his reign he achieved this with 300 of his students - almost all of these were women.

Inevitably the priesthood and the military chiefs got together and conspired to give Akhenaten a poison to kill him, thus thwarting his influence over the people. However, Akhenaten was immortal so they knew he would not actually die. They gathered three Nubian sorcerers to give Akhenaten a concoction which made him look dead. As soon as the royal doctor pronounced his 'death', they rushed his body to a special room where they had a sarcophagus waiting. They placed his body inside, put on the lid with a magical seal, and buried it in a well-hidden place. It would be 2000 years before a piece of the seal eroded and the spell was broken! Every effort was made to erase all evidence of his existence - a few statues are all that remain. But Akhenaten was unconcerned as he had lived his life, and knew that it would become encoded in the akashic records for all eternity. He also knew the country would fall back to their old ways. His legacy was the 300 immortal people who would carry on his teachings. These 300 Egyptians joined the Tat Brotherhood and waited from around 1350 BC to 500 BC - about 800 years. Then they migrated to a place called Masada, Israel, and formed the Essene Brotherhood. These 300 people became the 'inner circle', joined by other who became the 'outer circle'. Mary, mother of Yeshua, was one of these 300, and Joseph was part of the outer circle.

It was all part of the plan and was as it was meant to be...

I had been on the road for so long with Yeshua I had few belongings; just a few shawls to keep warm on the boat at night. Lazarus saddled up Eos, our donkey, and tied on our bundles of mattresses, blankets, food and water. Joseph led the way with Eos; I followed behind accompanied by Mother Mary and Mary Salome, (who had never left my side since I had decided to follow Yeshua), Martha (my sister), her maid Martilla and Maximin. My brother Lazarus stayed behind to settle the family estate and would join us as soon as he could.

We reached Joppa in the early evening. We had rested during the heat of the day - Joseph had found shade under olive trees away from the side of the road. He was keen for us to stay out of sight - the Romans may have put a price on our heads and he wasn't going to take any chances.

I smelt the sea before I saw it. The cobalt blue Mediterranean sea was glistening in the evening light. Joppa sat on a sandy promontory between Caesarea and Gaza, and was the chief sea port in Judea. Founded by the

Phoenicians, it had become a Jewish town in the second century BCE.

Joseph found lodgings for us near the harbour. We only needed two rooms, one for the men and one for the women. I unrolled my mattress and slipped into the welcome oblivion of deep sleep. The next thing I knew was Martha gently waking me in the morning; she had already been to the market to buy provisions for our voyage to Alexandria. Meanwhile, Joseph had found a trading ship bound for Alexandria that day, so we bade farewell to Lazarus. He would return to Bethany and join us in Alexandria as soon as he could. Joseph thought the weather seemed settled for the next day or two. The prevailing Etesian northern winds were blowing at 15-20 knots - this would mean we should make 5 knots with a comfortable sea motion as we were travelling south west. With luck, we could sail the 260 miles to Alexandria within forty eight hours.

I remember little of the voyage; I was physically and emotionally exhausted after the events of the last week. The motion of the boat meant I dozed much of the day, but then I would dream of Yeshua and wake with a jolt as it all came flooding back to me... in the moments that I was awake I gazed at the horizon or into the sky, trying to picture Yeshua's face in my mind - how he used to smile at me, not how he was at the end. At night, the two Marys, Martha and I would huddle down together and Joseph would cover us with blankets. The gentle rolling motion of the boat together with the sound of the waves lapping on the wooden hull was comforting and soporific - we slept and slept.

CODEX II: THE GOSPEL OF THOMAS

Jesus said to his disciples, "Compare me to something and tell me what I am like".

Simon Peter said to him, "You are like a just messenger". Matthew said to him, "You are like a wise philosopher". (Judas) Thomas said to him, '"Teacher my mouth is utterly unable to say what you are like".

Jesus said, "I am not your teacher. Because you have drunk, you have become intoxicated from the bubbling spring that I have tended." And he took him (Judas), and withdrew, and spoke three sayings to him.

When (Judas) Thomas came back to his friends, they asked him "What did Jesus say to you?". (Judas) Thomas said to them, '"If I tell you one of the sayings he spoke to me, you will pick up rocks and stone me, and fire will come from the rocks and consume you..."

The Gospel according to Thomas

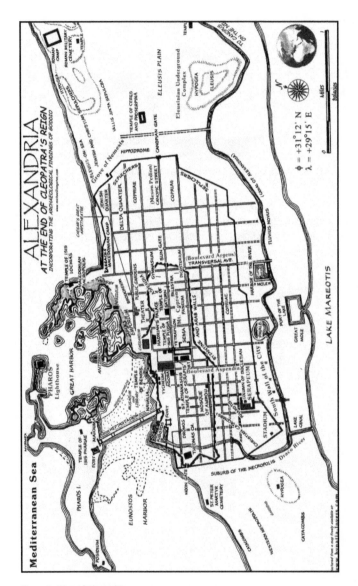

Figure 1 : Map of Alexandria

CHAPTER II

April 33 CE: Alexandria

After two days and two nights at sea I awoke to see the lighthouse, Pharos, towering above the water some 400 hundred feet high! Constructed in granite and limestone blocks faced with white marble, it had taken twelve years to build and was a sight to behold! No wonder it was one of the seven ancient wonders of the world! During the day a great mirror reflected the rays of the sun out to sea. At night a bonfire was lit and the mirror reflected the firelight out to sea.

We were still 30 miles or so from Alexandria, but there it was, its fire at the top, guiding us and ships from all over the western and middle-eastern world into the safety of one of the two harbours.

We entered via the Great Harbour. The Palace buildings and Caesarium were the next feast for our eyes - white marble glistening majestically in the sunlight. Under the Ptolemy Kingdom, which reigned from 332 - 30 BCE, the enormous wealth of Egypt had been used to construct these monumental buildings. Each successive King adding a new residence, so the palace area occupied a third of the city.

Our captain lowered the mainsail to reduce our speed and one of the crew peered over the bow to look for rocks and coral. The captain gripped the wheel with his eyes keenly set on the marker buoys. Joseph said many a ship had been wrecked on the shores of Pharos and been easy pickings for the inhabitants of Port of Pirates.

The harbour entrance was equally hazardous with ships grounding on the needle sharp coral reefs lying just below the surface. A sudden squall or becalming could spell disaster for a vessel and her crew - the captain could not relax until the anchor was down.

Having safely negotiated the shallow water, one of the crew dropped the mainsail and we came alongside the quay. Two other crew members threw mooring lines to helpful locals standing on the quay. After they had secured the lines they looked to the captain for a tip. Joseph helped us ashore with our belongings.

It was a fine sunny morning and the seafront was just as I remembered it - vibrant, colourful, bustling, noisy - everyone in great haste. Fishing boats unloading their nets in time for the morning market - this was the busiest time of day for Alexandria.

We made our way to the great synagogue in the Jewish quarter in the north east of the city. This was known as the Delta quarter. The Septuagint, a Greek translation of the Hebrew Bible (the Torah and other writings), was produced here. The synagogue was vast, a kind of basilica mentioned in the Talmud as 'Israel's glory'. There were seventy one golden thrones, one for each of the elders of the Great Sanhedrin, each worth twenty one talents* of gold, with a wooden platform in the middle. The minister of the synagogue stood on this platform with flags in his hands. When it was time for the congregation to utter 'Amen', the minister would wave his flags!

Worship and study were not the only things to take place at the synagogue. Along the colonnaded sides of the huge central hall, craftsmen did business and socialized. This is where Joseph enquired about lodgings. Alexandria was a cosmopolitan city with many people passing through so Joseph was able to quickly arrange this. We were introduced to an Alexandrian Jew called Benjamin, who was widowed and in his fifties. He had kind eyes set in a lined brown face and looked older than his years. He said he would be grateful of the company and extra income.

We rented two rooms; one for the women, myself, the two Marys, Martha and her handmaiden Martilla, and one for Joseph and Maximin. The rooms were sparse, but we had our own mattresses which we rolled out at night and put away in the morning.

There was a small, shady, walled courtyard at the rear of the house which Benjamin said we were welcome to use. We had access to a kitchen where Benjamin's maid, Photini would prepare our breakfast and a simple evening meal. Photini laid out bread, olives and fruit every morning and in the evenings we had supper with Benjamin. I told him all about Yeshua and how we intended to carry on his teachings. He had many questions and was intrigued.

We had fresh water! What luxury! The Ptolemies had dug a canal to draw

* 1 talent (33kg) of gold would be worth over £1 million today!

fresh water from the Canopic branch of the Nile, about twenty-seven kilometres south-east of Alexandria. It was stored in underground cisterns in the city. The rich had their own cisterns below their private homes, whereas the poor had to fetch their water from open canals unprotected from contamination.

After a good night's rest I took great delight in regaling the history of Alexandria to the others and giving them a guided tour! Joseph knew it well of course, but still accompanied us - as my 'earth angel' he wouldn't let me out of his sight! Martilla's eyes were out on stalks! I remember being equally overwhelmed by the sights when I first came six years ago...

Alexandria was founded by Alexander the Great in 331 BC. It was to be the Hellenistic centre of Egypt, linking Greece with the rich Nile valley. Sheltered by the island of Pharos, just west of the 'Canopic' mouth of the river Nile, it was the best site on the Egyptian coast. Fresh water would be in abundant supply from a canal from the Nile and Lake Mareotis.

Alexander the Great's chief architect for the project was Dinocrates. A few months after the foundation of Alexandria, Alexander left Egypt for the East and never returned to his city. Illness resulted in his death at the age of thirty two. In a struggle with other successors of Alexander, his general, Ptolemy (who would become Ptolemy I of Egypt) succeeded in bringing Alexander's body to Alexandria. His tomb became a famous destination for ancient travellers, including Julius Caesar. Egypt was ruled by the Ptolemies from 305-30 BCE.

Alexandria became the centre of commerce between Europe and the Arabian and Indian East. In just one century, Alexandria had become the largest city in the world, second only to Rome in importance.

In the third century BC, the rulers of the New Kingdom used the wealth generated by Egypt's empire to fund huge building projects both in Alexandria and throughout the country. The Serapeum was built under Ptolemy I.

The end of the New Kingdom was marked by the loss of Egyptian influence abroad and a gradual decline in central authority. Against this background of political disunity, a series of foreign powers came to dominate Egypt, culminating with the Roman conquest in 30 BCE. Octavian, who later became the first Roman emperor Augustus, defeated Queen Cleopatra VII of Egypt and her Roman lover Antony. Egypt became a province of the Roman Empire.

Hippopotami, waterfowl, lotus flowers, crocodiles and the Nile itself conjured an exotic vision of Egypt for the Greeks and Romans, as they had done even before the days the pharaohs created this unique kingdom.

The Musaeum and Library of Alexandria were built under Ptolemy II. They became a renowned centre for Hellenistic learning. They were connected with one another and the palaces by long colonnades of the most costly marble from the Egyptian quarries, and adorned with obelisks and sphinxes taken from the Pharaonic cities. The Musaeum succeeded the once renowned college of Heliopolis as the University of Egypt. It contained a great hall (or banqueting room) where the professors dined communally, an exterior corridor for exercise and walking lectures, a theatre where public disputations and scholastic festivals were held, chambers for the different professors, botanical gardens with tropical flora, and a menagerie! It was divided into four principal sections; poetry, mathematics, astronomy and medicine.

It attracted scholars and philosophers from all over the world, analogous to a modern university. Up to a thousand scholars could be in residence at any one time - fed and watered with no obligation to pay taxes - they could just study!

It was rumoured the Library had around 400,000 books or scrolls in their stores. All visiting ships had to relinquish any books; these were then copied. The originals were taken and the copies returned to the owner! Part of this unrivalled collection was kept in the Serapeum; some 200,000 volumes collected by the kings of Pergamus, and presented by M. Antonius to Cleopatra.

Sadly, the Library was badly damaged by a fire set by Julius Caesar in 48 BC. The Serapeum was considered the daughter of the Library of Alexandria. It was built on the acropolis of Alexandria, a rocky plateau overlooking land and sea, the largest and most magnificent of all temples in the Greek quarter of Alexandria. It was elevated on a great platform, over a hundred steps high. Made of gleaming white marble and painted and gilded on the inside, it was a sight to behold!

In an effort to unite the religions and cultures of the Egyptians and Greeks, Ptolemy I invented a new god, Serapis. He took a cult statue from Sinope and brought it to Alexandria, saying that he had been bidden to do so in a dream. Local legend claims the statue hopped in the Alexandrian ship after the locals proved unwilling to part with it! Upon its arrival in Alexandria, two religious experts employed by the king declared the statue to be Serapis. Serapis was a combination of the traditional Egyptian gods Osiris and Apis, sprinkled with the attributes of the Hellenistic gods Zeus, Helios, Dionysus, Hades and Asklepius. Serapis was thus a supreme god of divine majesty and the sun (Zeus and Helios), fertility (Dionysos), the underworld and afterlife (Hades, Apis and Osiris). His connection to the afterlife and fertility were considered the most important. The statue of Serapis was so large each hand seemed to touch the wall on either side!

The cult statue of Serapis was in classical Greek form, with no animal-headed Egyptian characteristics that would have been off-putting to the Greeks. Its iconography was that of Hades - wearing a robe, Greek hairstyle and beard - with a basket of grain on his head symbolizing fertility and his connection with Osiris, god of grain.

There was already precedent for combining Egyptian gods into one. Apis, the bull, was regarded as the incarnation of Osiris, and Osiris was sometimes called 'the bull of the west'. The statue of Apis was made of many precious materials and was dark blue in colour.

Temple officials employed some clever techniques to seduce the crowds. A hidden magnet was fixed in the ceiling above the statue, so that Serapis appeared to rise up and remain suspended in the air! A small window was strategically positioned so that a beam of sunlight touched the lips of Serapis in a kiss of renewal.

Shaped like a Macedonian soldier's cloak, the city was walled and occupied an area of about four square miles - its length from east to west was nearly four miles; its breadth from north to south nearly a mile. The interior was laid out like parallelograms; the streets crossed one another at right angles, and were all wide enough to admit both wheel carriages and foot passengers. Two grand thoroughfares nearly bisected the city, running in straight lines to its four principal gates.

The longest, 40 stadia* in length, ran from the Canobic gate in the east to that of the Necropolis in the west. The shorter, 7-8 stadia in length, ran from the Gate of the Moon in the north to the Gate of the Sun in the south.

Lake Mareotis lay to the south, just beyond the city walls. There were two harbours; the Great Harbour to the east and Eunostos Harbour to the west. Pharos Island was a dazzling white calcareous rock and home to the towering lighthouse. The island broke the force of the north wind and occasional high floods of the Mediterranean. Pharos Island was joined to the mainland by a man made Heptastadium, measuring seven stadia, (or three quarters of a mile).

Around 500,000 Greek, Jewish and Egyptian people, not including slaves, lived in five quarters, named after the first five letters of the Greek alphabet; Alpha, Beta, Gamma, Delta and Epsilon. The Jews occupied two of these quarters and represented the largest Jewish community in the world.

Practical reasons determined where individual Jewish families would live and work. Artisans clustered alongside fellow craftsmen in the same trade, such as glassmaking, so that a whole district would be known by what goods were produced there. Alexandria produced a number of export goods, including, paper, flax, jewellery and cosmetics. Men of means lived close to the city centre so they could walk from place to place, or be carried by slaves on foot. Houses were colonnaded, with separate men's and women's quarters. Chambers had golden ceilings. Some had stables for the owner's horses. Fierce dogs would guard the owners' properties. Exotic pets could be heard - parrots and talking crows! Around 400 of these homes belonged to the Jewish community but the majority of the non-elite lived farther away from the city centre in their own districts. The streets narrowed down into winding alleyways and people lived cheek by jowl in the densely populated poorer areas.

Like Jerusalem, the Jewish district, or Delta, had walls and gates of its own which at times were highly necessary for security. Frequent hostilities raged between the Alexandrian Greeks and Jews, inflamed both by political jealousy and religious hatred. The Jews were governed by their own Sanhedrin or senate, and their own national laws. In 31 BCE, Augustus Caesar granted to the Alexandrian Jews equal privileges with their Greek fellow citizens.

---

* 1 stadia is equivalent to 565 feet or 1/10 of a mile

However, any concessions or privileges were frequently overturned or annulled by successive Roman emperors. The Jewish people were always considered interlopers by the Greeks; they were not entitled to citizenship, socially desirable but equally important, exempt from paying taxes.

Great sophistication and palatial homes stood alongside slavery and despair. I had seen some terrible sights in the agora. There was a lunatic named Carabas, not angry or violent, but gentle and quiet. He spent day and night in the streets naked in the heat of the day and the cold nights, taunted by the children for their amusement.

I saw raw brutality as well. People lived in fear of the tax collectors, who were not bureaucrats but thugs and bullies. Rome demanded a princely sum, and did not care by what means it was procured. Some of the men who could not pay would take flight, convinced the tax-collector would go to any ends to extort the money. The tax-collector then seized their closest family members - their wives, children and parents. He tortured them in order to extort the money from them, or to find the fugitives' whereabouts. But they were unable to supply either, and so he filled a large basket with sand and, having hung this enormous weight by ropes around their necks, set them in the middle of the market-place in the open air. They sank under the stress of the sun and the shame of being seen by the passers-by with the weights suspended on them.

This spectacle in the middle of the agora instilled so much fear that others committed suicide by sword, poison or hanging to avoid a similar ordeal for themselves and their families. Those who showed themselves to be friends automatically became liable for the debts. Tax-collectors had been known to continue whipping the corpses after the victims have died. They defended their actions by explaining it would incite the relatives to pay to have the bodies released.

The agora itself was an exciting but potentially dangerous place. Roman officials might come sweeping through in their chariots without warning, and the crowds would have to back away and clear a pathway for them as they went by. Beasts of burden also carried their loads through the agora on their way to the market stalls. Apart from the danger of being trampled underfoot, there was always the risk of an unprovoked personal assault. Fights were commonplace. The pent-up anger of people living in poverty and overcrowding led to frequent outbreaks of violence, with stoning being the most common outlet for rage in Alexandria and other cities of the ancient world.

My previous time in Alexandria seemed another lifetime now...I had changed. I was having a child - Yeshua's child! And I wanted to be somewhere quiet where I could listen to him. I was on a mission - I had work to do...

That night I dreamt I lived in a small community on the shores of Lake Mareotis. When I awoke I knew this was where I wanted to live...I needed to speak to Joseph! It had to be simple. Yeshua had taught me how to live simply. My days of expensive clothes and jewellery were a distant memory...

I went directly to Joseph and he said we had better start looking immediately; find out what land was available and what was affordable. Lazarus would be arriving from Bethany soon and we would have ample funds for the land purchase, materials and labour.

CODEX III: THE DIALOGUE OF THE SAVIOUR

Mary utters words of wisdom

Mary said, "So,
The wickedness of each day is sufficient.
Workers deserve their food.
Disciples resemble their teachers."
She spoke this utterance as a woman who understood everything.

Mary and the Other Disciples Discuss True Life with the Master

Mary said, "I want to understand all things, just as they are."
The master said, "Whoever seeks life, this is their wealth. For the world's
rest is false, and its gold and silver are deceptive."...

Judas asked, "Tell me, master, what is the beginning of the way?"

He said, "Love and goodness. If one of these had existed among the
rulers, wickedness would never have come to be."

Conclusion

As for you, work hard to rid yourselves of anger and jealousy, and strip
yourselves of your works, and do not... reproach... For I say to you... you
receive... many... one has sought, having found true life. This person will
attain rest and live forever. I say to you, watch yourselves, so that you may
not lead your spirits and your souls into error.

CHAPTER III

Lake Mareotis: June 33 CE

The entrance to Lake Mareotis was a finger of the lake which actually breached the southern wall, just a 30 minute walk from our lodgings. Canals also ran through the city joining the lake to the western harbour in the Mediterranean. The lake was vast - around 100 square miles in area with eight islands, all inhabited. The part of the lake directly south of the city was a busy shipping conduit. Traffic from the East that reached the Nile passed by the canal to Lake Mareotis, and onto Alexandria and the Western Empire.

We exited the city via the Moon Gate, and headed south west. The western end of the lake became more placid. Here were the summer estates of wealthy Alexandrians. The air was an admirable temperature from the continual breezes which came from the lake and fell into the sea; the breezes from the lake being light, and those which fell into the sea being heavy, the mixture of which produced a most healthy atmosphere. This region was famous for its wine produced here.

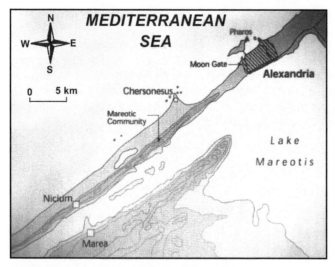

Figure 2: Map showing location of Lake Mareotis community

The larger estates gradually died out and we had been walking for two to three hours when we found the perfect spot on a low hill! A 30 metre high ridge to the north provided a backdrop and sloped gently down to the shores of the lake. So when the Mediterranean floods came we wouldn't be under water! It was relatively safe with houses built in the fields and villages surrounding it on all sides.

And there was fresh running water! There was a spring at the foot of the hill, water gurgling gently out of the ground through reeds and plants. It flowed down a channel to the lake. Papyrus plants grew abundantly in the marshy borders beside the lake - papyrus was one of Alexandria's main products, 'The Strip' gave its name to a particular type of papyrus. Palm trees swayed gently in the breeze - they would afford welcome shade in the heat of the day.

Joseph staked out an area of five acres or so; he said we would need to be fenced in - there were reports of bandits in the area and he would not be happy leaving me to the mercy of wild dogs and bandits! I was so excited!

We returned to Alexandria and I sketched a plan of what I wanted. A cluster of twenty cabins with an adjoining courtyard, cooking area, eatery and meeting hall. As our numbers swelled, we could add more cabins! Joseph went to the authorities to find out who owned the land and arrange the purchase. Nobody wanted it as it was considered too remote for people working in Alexandria. The exact reason I wanted it! This also made it affordable - an added bonus!

Joseph organized everything with the carpenters. Joseph was a businessman and I was very grateful for his expertise. He was fair and the workmen respected him. They worked hard and the buildings only took six weeks from start to finish!

When I wasn't inspecting the building of our little community, I busied myself by preaching in the Agora. The two Marys were always with me, my guardian angels! This is what Yeshua had asked us to do - teach the Way of the Heart. And yet we saw some terrible sights which would make me weep. Yeshua would have been so angry at the injustices and inequality we saw every day. The poor lived in fear. Stonings could take place at any time due to the tension amongst the people, particularly between the Greeks and the Jews - there was no love lost there.

Alexandria was a wonderful city, if you were wealthy... slaves could be bought or claimed in war. Sometimes their fortunes changed and they were able to buy their liberty, some of them would even buy their own slaves, but then something would go wrong - an unpaid debt, or medical bill, and they would have to return to life as a slave. Old men with wizened faces looked hunched and old beyond their years from carrying loads, and even their owners, on their backs. Life expectancy for these people rarely exceeded forty. At least the slaves of the wealthy lived in habitable conditions, whereas the poor were left to live like sewer rats in insect infested detritus.

We moved to Lake Mareotis in July 33 CE. I was seven months pregnant by then, desperate to move out of Alexandria and have a home again. Benjamin and Photini helped us move our belongings. The work men too. Benjamin was sorry to see us leave, but promised to visit us - we weren't very far away after all!

Photini was uncharacteristically quiet as our agreed date of departure approached; she would have liked to come with us, but felt honour bound to stay and take care of Benjamin. As she said herself, he had been very good to her and she owed it to him. As I hugged her goodbye, I told her she could visit anytime and maybe one day, when she was free, she could come and live with us. This gave her hope, and cheered her considerably. Thankfully it was true, albeit not as soon as she would have liked...

Our way of living at the community had to be simple. Falsehood is the foundation of pride, whereas truth is the origin of simplicity. From falsehood comes every variety of evil and wickedness, whereas from truth comes every imaginable abundance of good things both human and divine.

All the wooden cabins were for sole occupancy; they were identical in size measuring 15 feet by 15 feet, with a private courtyard. They were plain in style giving shelter against the heat of the sun and the cold night air. They were far enough apart to give each occupant privacy, but near enough to be of assistance if there was an unwelcome intrusion. In each cabin was a sacred shrine which was called the Holy Place, in which to retire by oneself and perform all the mysteries of a holy life, bringing in nothing, neither meat, nor drink, nor any luxuries. An oil lamp and candles were supplied and writing materials on request. We all studied the laws and sacred oracles of God enunciated by the holy prophets, composed our own writings and wrote songs and hymns.

This gave us an imperishable recollection of God, so even in our dreams we were privy to the beauty of the divine virtues and divine powers. Many would speak in their sleep, divulging the celebrated doctrines of the sacred philosophy.

We attracted wealthy men and women from Alexandria who happily gave up their property to relatives to join our community and live a strict ascetic life. We did not drink alcohol or eat meat and for six days a week, meditated upon God in solitary confinement.

We had community prayers at dawn and sunset, with every hour in between devoted to studying and writing. When the sun rose, we prayed to God that the happiness of the coming day be real, so that our minds were filled with heavenly light. And when the sun was setting, we prayed that our souls, being lightened of the burden of our outward senses, may be able to find trust in our own chamber.

Our staple diet was salted bread cooked in the outside oven and spring water. We resisted those feelings which nature has made mistresses of the human race, namely hunger and thirst. So we ate only as far as not to be hungry, and drank enough to escape from thirst, avoiding satiety, as an enemy of both body and soul.

I was heavily pregnant and had to take care of my body, so I would eat a little when I rose at dawn, and then not again until dusk when I finished writing.

Many of the ancient scriptures and philosophy were in allegorical form; shrouded in myths. These allegories were contemplated and studied at great length as possible symbolisation of a secret meaning of nature. Interpretation was multi-layered, depending on where the reader was placed in his or her spiritual development. When Yeshua was alive he often spoke in parables, and he frequently said his teachings were for those who had eyes to see and ears to hear.

Some of the men, with a fervent desire for knowledge, would fast for three or even six days - so delighted when supplied with doctrines in all possible wealth and abundance, sitting like grasshoppers, feeding happily on air!

The semi-fasting heightened my meditative state. Food just made me sleepy. I wrote all day every day, six days a week. The words flowed with no effort, not from the mind, but from the heart. I would wake in the night with Yeshua's voice in my head, urging me to arise and start writing... I wrote in Greek and Mary Salome, Mother Mary and Martha would make copies for me, so we had four copies of everything I wrote. These were important words from Yeshua - their preservation was important for the survival of humanity now and in the future. This was my mission now. We didn't have Yeshua with us in the flesh, but his teachings continued...

The Sabbath was the occasion for an assembly in the great hall. The hall was lined with benches, and we filed onto these according to age, and in silence, keeping our hands inside our garments, with our right hand on our chest and the left hand by our side. Men and women did not sit together. A chest-high screen divided the room in two with the women behind the men. Both men and women delivered the homily at worship. We took it in turns! We had no positions of office - no bishop or Sanhedrin!

Our clothing was restricted to two garments to protect us from extreme cold and heat. A cloak of shaggy hide for the winter, and a thin mantle or linen shawl for the summer. We also had a white gown kept for festivals and special ceremonies.

We celebrated Jewish festivals, but the most important one was Pentecost. One of the older members, a man or woman, was appointed president before the ceremony began. We would dress in our ceremonial robes and file in with our right hand on our heart and our left arm by our side. Then it was time for an opening prayer, with our faces and hands in the prayer position raised towards heaven. Then we reclined in order of seniority, oldest first, women on one side and men on the other, on the papyrus couches we had made from planks nailed together and covered with papyrus reeds.

After what I had witnessed in the agora I was opposed to slavery on all grounds, so our attendants were younger members of the community.

Before the meal there was a programme directed by the president - a discussion of questions arising from the scriptures or tractates, either ancient ones or those I had written or transmitted. The 'president' repeated the questions slowly so everyone could understand, speaking with great powers of reasoning and prudence, explaining with minute accuracy the precise meaning of the laws, which penetrated through our hearing into our souls. Everyone listened in rapt silence, showing our assent or understanding by nods of the head, or the eager look of eyes. The end of the homily was greeted with rapt applause! Following this, we sang hymns, both well known or of our own composition, and the whole assembly joined in the choruses. The meal of bread and water followed. The spring water was warmed for the older members, to ease the digestion of the salted bread which was sometimes seasoned with hyssop.

After the meal the men and women would form two choruses. Spontaneous dancing ensued and the choirs melded into one. Singing and dancing would continue into dawn, the choristers ecstatic in sober drunkenness. We would spin around the floor, faster and faster, weaving in and out of one another, but never clashing, like planets orbiting around the sun. We were outside of time. Spinning frees the soul, where there is no mind. Everything is energy, and the mind likes to block the energy because it likes to be in control and stops us remembering who we are. When the soul is free, the third eye can open and enables inner vision.

As the sun rose, we turned to the east and stretched our hands towards the heavens in prayer, just as the day had begun.

The festival ended, and we returned to our cabins to resume our studies *living in the soul alone.*

This was the first Christian community. I felt Yeshua would be proud of us...

CODEX III: EUGNOSTOS THE BLESSED

Eugnostos the blessed, to those who are his.

Greetings. I want you to know that all people born from the foundation of the world until now are of dust. They have inquired about God, who he is and what he is like, but they have not found him. The wisest of people have speculated about truth on the basis of the order of the universe, but their speculation has missed truth. Philosophers voice three different opinions about the order of the universe, and they disagree with each other. Some of them say that the universe has governed itself, others say that divine forethought has governed it, and still others that fate has been in charge. All these opinions are wrong... Any life that comes from itself is empty, made by itself. Forethought is foolish. Fate is senseless.

Whoever can come with another option to confess the God of truth and agree about everything concerning him, is immortal while living among mortal people.

The One Who Is

The One Who Is is ineffable. From the foundation of the world, no power, no authority, no creature, no nature has known the One Who Is.
Only the One Who Is knows itself.

CHAPTER IV

The arrival of the Apostles: August 33 CE

Both great joy and sadness accompanied the arrival of the apostles. Matthew, Simon Peter, Simon the Zealot, James son of Alpheus, Andrew, Thomas, Bartholomew, Philip, James son of Zebedee, Thaddaeus, Luke and Mark finally joined our community. I had been expecting them of course, that was the plan we made in Jerusalem - for them to join me here in Alexandria, as soon as we had somewhere for them to stay. There were also two men I had not met before - they had come to Christ after I left Bethany; Paul and Matthias.

But all had not gone as we had planned... we wept as they related events leading to blessed Stephen's stoning in Jerusalem on 3rd August. Stephen was one of Yeshua's seventy two disciples and one of the seven deacons the apostles had ordained for ministry. Stephen, full of grace and fortitude, did great wonders and signs among the people. The Jews, being jealous of him, wanted to discredit him and find him guilty. They went about this in three ways; by argument, by producing false witnesses, and subjecting him to torture. But he won the arguments, convicted the false witnesses, and triumphed over his torturers, and in each encounter aid was given from our Lord.

In the first, the Holy Spirit aided him with divine wisdom. In the second, it was his face, like the face of an angel, that terrified the false witnesses. In the third, Christ himself appeared, ready to give aid and to strengthen the martyr.

As they were stoning him, he prayed for himself - that his passion might not be prolonged and their guilt thereby augmented, and for them - that they would not be held guilty of this sin. As a volley of stones hit his body, he called upon God and prayed, "Lord Jesus, receive my spirit." And, falling to his knees, he cried out with a loud voice, saying "Lord, lay not this sin to their charge, because they know not what they do!".

In this the martyr imitated Yeshua, who in his passion prayed for himself, saying, "Into my hands I commend my spirit" and for his executioners, "Father, forgive them, for they know not what they do". And when Stephen had made his prayer, he fell asleep in the Lord. Gamaliel and Nicodemus, who stood up for the Christians in all the councils of the Jews, buried him in a plot of land that belonged to Gamaliel, and mourned greatly over him.

A violent persecution broke out against the Christians in Jerusalem as Stephen, one of their leaders, had been killed. The rest were hotly pursued and scattered throughout the territory of the Jews. The apostles, who were braver than the others, followed the Lord's command to them: "If they persecute you in one town, flee to another." And so they came to Lake Mareotis.

But they had news of a second tragedy. John and Judas were not with them. Peter told me that John had stayed in Jerusalem. My suspicions were he did not want to join a community led by a woman, but Peter denied this was the case. I think he was sparing my feelings. And where was Judas? Peter could not look me in the eye - he stared at the ground and dissolved into tears. He collapsed onto the ground and begged for forgiveness - forgiveness from me and forgiveness from Yeshua.

I silently feared the worst, rooted to the spot as I waited for him to tell me what happened. I knew already, as Judas had foretold his own death, but I still wanted to hear it. Peter related that tension was high after the crucifixion, and an argument had broken out between the apostles. Judas had claimed that Yeshua had asked him to betray him to the authorities and how it broke his heart to do it. He went onto say that Yeshua felt Judas was the only one who understood and would comply with his wishes. At this, hot-headed Peter lost his temper, grabbed Judas and threw him to the ground.

"No, you are a traitor! Yeshua would never have asked you! You think you are so special!"

Not one of them believed poor Judas...

Maybe it was the beatific look on Judas' face as he lay on the ground, in complete submission like a wounded animal, or a man who knew his fate and accepted it. As Yeshua had done. It was John who threw the first rock, and he who incited the others to join in. All the angst, fear and grief they all felt burst forth and was vented on poor innocent Judas! They hailed stones at him in a frenzy until he no longer moved or cried out in pain - I had witnessed it on several occasions in the agora in Alexandria so I knew exactly what Judas had gone through. I wept for poor Judas. Then in shocked silence they buried his body, digging the earth with their bare hands, the realisation of what they had done dawning on each and every one of them. Even if Judas had been a traitor, which he wasn't, they had murdered in the name of our Lord, against everything Yeshua had taught us.

They were all to blame, but John felt responsible as the ringleader and could not face me. He journeyed alone to Ephesus to preach the gospel - he never came to Lake Mareotis, it was many years before I saw him again..

I embraced them all one by one - Yeshua's message was the Way of the Heart and he would have forgiven them, so who was I to pass judgement? I was crying inside though - I loved Judas as a brother.

I prayed for them all, especially John. He was passionate, quick to anger and believed he was right. A dangerous combination. He would have to live with his actions for the rest of his days - he was a good man, who had killed in a moment of madness.

As soon as they had bathed in the lake and been assigned their cabins I told them to prepare for a baptism ceremony. A new beginning. No more killing in the name of God. How many times has that happened in history? No wonder people are suspicious of religion!

The baptism, or five seals ceremony, transforms the initiate by way of a rebirth in the Light and a means for immortality of the soul. It was attended by the whole community on the shores of the lake.

The five "seals" are symbolically performed by the five triads of fifteen angels; baptism in living water, donning of the ceremonial robe, being anointed with oil (symbolizing kingship), glorification and finally a 'snatching away' or experience of an ecstatic visionary ritual at the end of the ceremony.

The initiate would enter the water naked and be immersed five times. I would ask each initiate to clasp his or her hands and stretch them forward in a circle, symbolizing their soul, which we believe is spherical in shape. I would then say the following:

"I baptise you in the name of the Father, Mother and Son, and the angels MIKHEUS, MIKHAR, MNESINOUS, and SESENGENPHARANGES (a spirit/angel who presides over the 'baptism of the living'). Repeat after me 'I renounce the Archons and the Demiurge'.

The initiate would then don his ceremonial robe on the shore and the ceremony would continue there. I would continue:

"And I deliver him to those who give robes - AMMON, ELASSO, AMENAI - and they cover him with a robe from the robes of the Light; and I deliver him to the baptizers, and they baptize him - MIKHEUS, MIKHAR, MNESINOUS - and they immerse him in the Water of Life. And I deliver him to those who enthrone - BARIEL, NOUTHAN, SABENAI - and they enthroned him from the Throne of Glory. And I deliver him to those who glorify - ARIOM, ELIEN, PHARIEL - and they glorify him with the glory of the Fatherhood. And those who snatch away snatch away - KAMALIEL, ABRASAX, SAMBLO and the servants of the great holy luminaries - and they take him into the light-place of this Fatherhood. And he receives the five seals from the Light of the Mother, Protennoia, and it is granted for him to partake of the mystery of knowledge, and become a Light in Light."

For this is the true baptism, into which members of the All descend and come into being, and redemption takes place in God the Father, the Son and the Holy Spirit, after confession of faith has been made in those names. And whoever believes in their reality will obtain salvation, by attaining in an invisible way, the Father, the Son and the Holy Spirit.

This kind of baptism is called the *garment* that is worn by the ones who have received redemption and not taken off. It is also called *the confirmation of truth* which never fails its stability. It is called *silence* because of its tranquillity and unshakeability. It is called *the bridal chamber* because of the concord and inseparability of the ones he has known and have known him. It is called *the unsinking and fireless light*, not because it sheds light, but rather because those who wear it, and wear it well, are made into light. It is also called *the eternal life*, which means immortality. For how else can it be named than as the ALL? It transcends all words, all voice, all mind, all things and all silence.

I was just the messenger. Yeshua was able to give his initiates a vision of the heavenly spheres. This was in the form of an altered state of consciousness induced by the recitation of repetitive, hypnotic prayers and hymns, a technique described in Jewish mystical texts and Greek magical papyri. We could all feel Yeshua's presence - sometimes the initiate would be struck down and lie prostrate on the ground for a few minutes, sob, laugh, or just cry out ecstatically the Lord's praises, completely overcome with emotion.

It was an experience I felt privileged to be part of - for men and women to find that *divine spark* in themselves - to wake up and see there is so much more to life than transient pleasures of the flesh. To make an inward journey rather than looking outside. It was just the beginning of course, when we strip away the outer distractions, it is not always a vision of beauty when we go inside, there can be many complications ...discipline is required to stay on the path, but we were all there to support one another in times of doubt, which would occur for each and every one of us.

We attracted numerous visitors from Alexandria, drawn to our simple community life. We were known as the *Therapeutae* to the people of Alexandria. In Greek it means healing and worshipping - we served God and we were healers, healers of soul, mind and body.

For there are three kinds of medicine; some cures, some improves, some preserves. The heavenly physician has prescribed these three medicines for us. The medicine that *cures* diseases is *penance*, which cures every spiritual sickness. The Spirit of our Lord heals the contrite of heart, and sent me to preach deliverance to its captives. The medicine that *improves*, that is, increases good health, comes from observance of the counsels, for the counsels make people better and more perfect. For example, Yeshua said, "Sell all you have and distribute to the poor." The *preservative* medicine saves us from falling, by avoiding both the act of sinning and the company of sinners.

Men and women, rich or poor, all creeds and colour - all were made welcome. The wealthy were fascinated by our simple lifestyle - a stark contrast to the hedonistic lifestyle of the privileged in Alexandria. The poor were free - free from slavery and the daily grind of trying to feed their families, or evade the tax collector. Some stayed a few days, others weeks and even months.

Within a few months we were almost forty in number. The cabins were in high demand and we had to have more built! If community members were able to make a contribution or offering, they did, but it was not compulsory. They could not bring any property with them -some distributed their possessions amongst their family or sold them and made an offering to the community. We needed little money to run the community - enough to buy flour for the bread and oil for the lamps. Our only real expense was the purchase of materials for building the new cabins - our community was large enough by now that we could build them ourselves. Joseph handled our finances, when he wasn't sailing the oceans buying and selling tin.

I loved hearing of his travels on his return; he sailed to Greece, Gaul, Britain and even South America! He had taken Yeshua with him when he was a teenager - Yeshua had told me about visiting the tin mines in Cornwall and Joseph had regaled tales of a mystical place in England called Avalon*. He said he would take me one day...I would make that journey, but not with my beloved Yeshua.

I was happy here. My belly was swollen and my baby would be here soon - I did not wish to go anywhere - my work was here! We had everything we needed and more - we lived as kings and queens!

* Avalon is now known as Glastonbury

THE GOSPEL OF MARY

The Nature of Sin and Good

Peter said to him (Teacher): *"Since you have become the interpreter of the elements and the events of the world, tell us, what is the sin of the world?"*

The Teacher answered: *"There is no sin. It is you who make the sin exist, when you act according to the habits of your corrupted nature; this is where sin lies...this is why the Good has come into your midst. It acts together with the elements of your nature so as to reunite it with its roots".*

Then he continued: *"This is why you become sick, and why you die: it is the result of your actions; what you do takes you further away."*

Those who have ears let them hear.

Note: Of the 19 pages, the first six pages and four pages in the middle are missing.

Three fragmentary copies of The Gospel of Mary have been found in Egypt. The first is a version in Coptic, discovered in 1896 near the area of Achmim. Two additional fragments in Greek were found on the rubbish heap at Oxyrynchus.

CHAPTER V

September 14th 33 CE: The Birth of Sarah

The greatest challenge for children, especially girls, was survival. Disease, poverty and a widespread preference for sons over daughters all took their toll. One in three did not make their first birthday. Even if a child survived the trauma of birth, there was no guarantee the father would allow he or she to live. The Greeks called it ekthesis or 'putting outside'. A father could choose to leave a child on a dung heap, or in a place where it might be found by someone who would adopt it.

This seemed totally inconceivable to Yeshua and I. We both knew I was carrying a baby girl and had chosen a name together - Sarah. It means *princess* in Egyptian.

On 14th September 33 CE, our beautiful daughter entered this world! The two Marys attended me, of course. They massaged me with oils and prepared potions to relax my pelvic muscles to smooth her passage into this world. Mary Salome had been at the birth of Yeshua, attending his mother, Mother Mary, and now she was there for me. Perfect. I was spared a long and difficult labour, and she arrived in time for dawn prayers. She did not even cry! Mary Salome wrapped her in her shawl and placed her on my chest. I was delighted to see she had Yeshua's beautiful sapphire blue eyes - they would be a lifelong reminder of my beloved. I lost myself in her eyes, all I could see was pure innocence - no fear, guilt, shame or anger. She lay there gazing back at me, probably wondering which planet she had landed on! They say the eyes are the windows to the soul - she looked so wise, an old soul for sure!

She had a mop of dark brown hair and olive skin, smooth as marble! I looked up at the two Marys, standing over me, their faces full of sheer joy. Tears were rolling gently down Mother Mary's face as she gazed admiringly at her new granddaughter;

"She is the most beautiful baby I have ever set eyes on!", she gasped almost inaudibly "and she looks the image of Yeshua!". It was the happiest moment in my life... to give birth to my daughter, Yeshua's daughter. I let myself think for a second how perfect it would have been if Yeshua had still been with us...then I chided myself; this way of thinking would achieve nothing but self-pity.

But how he would have loved to be with us, holding his baby daughter in his arms - our baby daughter! Little Sarah!

The apostles were eager to meet the daughter of their Lord and they filed in for a brief visit. Peter led the way. One by one they held her and kissed her forehead. It was the happiest day for all of us who had been there on that Dark Day back in Jerusalem. No one had mentioned Judas since Peter had recounted what happened that day, but often what is unsaid is louder than any spoken words... it was always there, the 'elephant in the room'. Finally, something to celebrate and unite us all!

My recovery was swift with the help of the two Marys. They prepared different herbal infusions for me to drink and applied oils to speed my healing. I rested that day, nursing on demand. Peter had made her a crib but I wanted her next to me - I could not be parted from her. New-born babies sleep a great deal - she was so contented - she looked like she was dreaming of heaven and I wanted to be there with her...

Of course there was no nursery at our community, not even children, so Sarah stayed with me in my cabin for the rest of our stay at Lake Mareotis. It was not even discussed, just assumed that that would be the case.

During the day I would write, but at night I would just lie there, drinking in her beauty - I couldn't take my eyes off her, gazing at her purity and perfection with the aid of the moonlight, her tiny chest going up and down with her snuffly breath. I sang lullabies to her and regaled stories of her father from the moment she was born. No wonder she looked so happy!

On her third day Joseph baptized her. I felt very emotional, partly because my milk had come in and my hormones were raging. I wept with joy as I watched Joseph administer the five seals - Yeshua's presence was tangible. She didn't cry during the ceremony - she gurgled contentedly, and seemed to glow with light from the inside. Not surprising, as she was directly from heaven! Everyone was touched, it was an extremely intense experience for all of us present - she really was a gift from God! It was the proudest moment of my life, witnessing the baptism of my daughter!

If she was unsettled at all during the day I would strap her to my chest with my shawl, but she barely cried. Her tiny fingers would grasp my thumb as she fed eagerly. She would often fall asleep during or after being fed and I would lie her in her crib. I knew she was awake when I heard her gurgling with joy, telling the angels about her new life probably!

I didn't feel it was possible to love her more than I already did, but when she smiled at me for the first time my chest all but exploded! It was like a love affair! I hadn't felt this strength of emotion since I met Yeshua, which was very different of course, but equally giddying! Every mother knows this feeling; she thinks the birth of her baby is a miracle and her baby is the most beautiful baby in the world. Sarah was of course! I was not alone in this - the two Marys and Martha heartily agreed with me!

She thrived on love, light and milk and seemed to change almost daily. The weeks rolled into months, and she was keen to explore her environment. She was quickly able to focus on objects, support her head, roll over on the mattress, and then sit up without toppling over to one side or the other! Crawling introduced a whole new world to her, albeit within the confines of my cabin! It is such a joy to see the world through the eyes of a child; the sheer wonder and enthusiasm they express for the simplest thing - a leaf would be studied and meticulously inspected before being put in her mouth of course!

She seemed to sense the importance of what I was doing and was content to sit, play, crawl around or sleep in my cabin with me. If she was at all discontent during the day, one of the two Marys or Martha would instantly appear at my door and whisk her away. Mary Salome had no children of her own so was particularly attached to Sarah.

Peter loved making toys for her. First he made a rattle from wood collected from the lake shore, filled with dried seeds. She couldn't shake it to start with, but was soon able to grasp it whereupon it went straight into her mouth! Then a brightly coloured spinning top, she loved the way the colours all merged into one when it span. Then he made her a ball. I would put them away and retrieve them one at a time - she was so incredibly focused, and would study and play with whatever was in her hands for quite some time.

When she could sit up, at around six months, she would shake up and down with excitement when Peter or one of the others came to play with her. She didn't really need toys - she was fascinated by everything and anything - a leaf, a flower, a pebble from the shore, an insect. She squealed with delight when a grasshopper leapt across her path - she clearly thought that was miraculous!

Sarah started walking at ten months old, preferably holding Mary Salome or Martha's hand. She loved to toddle down to the lake shore and paddle in the shallow water desperately keen to explore her environment. She was never alone of course!

At a year old she could understand simple phrases, fixing me with her bright blue eyes, trying to figure out the mysteries of her rapidly expanding world! She was very intelligent - quick to grasp new experiences.

Oh I learnt so much from watching my beloved daughter grow. Her hair grew into soft but thick, dark brown curls which framed her round toddler face - my little cherub. But I had to remember she was not mine, she was on loan to me, I was only her custodian. I was her guide and here to keep her safe until she would make her own way in the world.. .not for a long time, I hoped. She was all I had to remind me of Yeshua.

She was wise beyond her years, respected all living things in a reasoned, mature manner - I was so proud of her, just sorry Yeshua wasn't here to share this with me. I don't remember her having a tantrum - why would she? Children live in the present and are totally immersed in whatever activity they are involved in, so if you decide it is time for them to do something else, eat, or get washed, for example, that leads to extreme frustration on their part. Time and patience... slowing down and doing things in their time, not yours! Such a great lesson! We were learning from one another! She lived in paradise surrounded by people who loved her - she had what all children need and should have - love and time.

I spoke to her in Hebrew and read to her from day one! Oh how she loved story time. I wrote in Greek so when she was old enough she would learn that too. I wanted her to have a first class education so I would look for a tutor for her; I had faith in one appearing when the time was right. I would teach her everything I had learnt at the Serapeum as one day she would be carrying on my work, my legacy.

THE GOSPEL OF MARY

The Saviour's Farewell

...The Blessed One greeted them all, saying,

"Peace be with you - may my Peace arise and be fulfilled within you! Be vigilant and allow no one to mislead you by saying:

'Here it is!' or 'There it is!'

For it is within you that the Son of Man dwells. Go to him, for those who seek him, find him. Walk forth, and announce the gospel of the Kingdom."

..."Impose no other law other than that which I have witnessed. Do not add more laws to those given by the Torah, lest you become bound by them." Having said all this, he departed.

CHAPTER VI

June 34 CE : Philo of Alexandria

In the first twelve months of living at the community I wrote codices II, III, and IV which comprised eleven tractates. They were all in Greek. I was not the only one writing - the apostles were also writing their own accounts of their life with Yeshua.

We wrote on papyrus in ink made from pulverized nut-galls (oak-galls), water, iron-sulphur and gum Arabic. The ink was kept in an ink horn.

Papyrus was originally imported into Greece through the Phoenician harbour of Byblos, and so Greeks began to call a book *biblios*. It now grew in abundance within a stone's throw and we collected it from the lake shore. Our pens were made from papyrus too, sharpened with a knife when they became blunt or dull. Papyrus was made from stalks of a reed plant to form sheets. We would normally write on one side, and they would be attached together to form long scrolls up to 100 feet long. Our preference was to make a codex. The word 'codex' comes from the Latin meaning 'tree trunk'. A codex was made by cutting a papyrus scroll into sheets, which were then stacked into a single pile, usually made up of at least 38 sheets. The pile of sheets was either sewed together, or fastened with leather thongs inserted in holes bored along one side. This produced a book of about 152 pages, which was finally placed inside a leather cover.

The Secret Book of *John* was my first transmission. For I was not writing these at all! The words just flowed from the heavens - from my beloved Yeshua. I assigned it to John as he was not with us. I thought he was ashamed to show his face but it later transpired he never saw Judas as an innocent party and he was angry with me. He didn't want to join a community led by a woman! Little did I know that this anger would turn into something more sinister and he would later ensure I was banished once and for all...

So why did I write under pseudonyms? Who would take any notice of a woman? It would be much later before I signed my own name - *The Gospel of Mary* which I wrote in 54CE.

Yeshua encoded *The Secret Book of John* with the use of allegory and myth. Yeshua said a myth is like a key that opens the most unsympathetic soul to the written word. These texts were to serve as inspiration, poetry and symbolism. They also had to withstand the passage of time, both physically and metaphorically. History often consisted of *truths* that became *stories*, whereas myths were *stories* that *symbolise* and had the power to become *truths*. For the *truth* is only the *truth* in the now, it is not set in stone. Even a stone erodes to dust.

The two Marys and Martha made three copies of each tractate (or gospel), all in Greek. *The Secret Book of John* appears in all three codices. The purpose of this was two-fold. The apostles would not be staying at our community indefinitely - Yeshua wanted us to 'spread the gospel', and it was our mission to start communities in other places and lands. We would start in Egypt, travelling up the Nile, looking for suitable locations close to living water but away from habitation, and then to foreign lands. We would be guided by Yeshua of course.

The other reason was for safe keeping. These were uncertain times. There was great unrest in Egypt and Judea, particularly where the Jewish population was concerned. In the Roman Empire the plight of the Jews was always subject to the whims of the current Roman emperor. I would have to think of somewhere to entrust these writings after my time on earth was over so they would be preserved for the future. For the future of humanity!

Our numbers continued to grow, and we were visited frequently by people either living in or passing through Alexandria. One man in particular would have an impact on our community, Philo of Alexandria. He would attend regularly on the Sabbath - he was truly fascinated with our way of life and studies - he was a philosopher and Orthodox Jew so it was baffling for him to come across a community led by a woman! Our place was in the home! He watched and was intrigued. Then one day we sat down together and he told me his story.

The single most powerful Jew in Alexandria was Alexander Lysimachus. He was in charge of collecting all customs due on goods imported from the East, and became one of the richest men in the ancient world. So powerful that he could marry one of his sons to the great granddaughter of Herod the Great.

Alexander had a younger brother, a man little interested in money, power and worldly affairs. His name was Julius Philo, and would become known as Philo of Alexandria.

Philo was born in 12 BCE into one of the wealthiest and more privileged Jewish families in the city. As such, he enjoyed many of the liberties of citizenship, and at 14 years of age was taken to the Serapeum, where a priest sheared his long childhood hair and enrolled him as an *ephebos* - a young man eligible to receive the most select education available. He then set out on the highly desirable *encyclia*, the secondary education that included grammar, rhetoric, music, dialectics, geometry and astronomy.

As a physical counterpart to these mental exertions, he was required to exercise in the great gymnasium, where he learned boxing and wrestling - the main sports of the day. He also practised the javelin, the discus, built up strength with the punching bag, and mixed with the other privileged youths who cooled their tired muscles in the fountains of the gymnasium's grounds. Outside his studies, he watched classical plays at the theatre, or observed politicians working the crowds. He and his friends also entertained themselves by betting on the outcome of the races in the hippodrome before retiring to their clubs for an evening of banqueting.

This regime was an entry into a life of great privilege. Philo, a believer in the Great Chain of Being that linked all living things in order from the lowliest animals (and humans) up to God, was certain he stood near the top. His time as an *ephebos* granted him the highly prized full citizenship of Alexandria - exemption from the Roman poll tax and the right to marry who he chose.

Philo was intrigued by our community which he termed *Therapeutae*, as we evidently practised an art of medicine superior to that in use in cities (for that only heals bodies, but ours heals souls which are under the master of a multitude of passions and vices inflicted upon them). We sought to deny the senses to find a pure spirituality serving the living God, honouring the elements earth, water, air and fire. Our members believed their mortal life had already come to an end, and in their desire for an immortal and blessed existence, willingly left their possessions to their relations, cheerfully giving up their inheritance. Carried away by great desire and a certain heavenly love and enthusiasm, we aimed at obtaining a sight of the living God.

Despite his education, philosophizing and strict attendance to the Great synagogue, something in Philo's life was clearly missing. Philo found something at our community which he had never experienced. He was tired of the hedonistic sights he had both experienced and witnessed in Alexandria, the debauchery and slavery to pleasures of the flesh. His visits became more frequent, although he never turned his back completely on his life in Alexandria. He said part of him would have loved to, as there was a time when he devoted all his waking hours to philosophy and contemplation. Mundane matters like food, clothing, glory and wealth were all within his grasp but did not inspire him. But that serenity did not last, and he was thrust into politics, as a well-connected Jew with influence. Alexandria was the granary of Egypt, it was in the Romans' interest that unrest was kept to a minimum and the economy would not suffer. The Romans sought his counsel frequently about how to deal with the continual scuffles and unrest between the Greeks and the Jews. He said it was like dealing with squabbling children, except worse, because they never grew out of it. It would dissipate for a while, giving him a respite for reflection, knowing that before long he would be assailed once again by waves of people and affairs.

I loved talking to Philo - he was so intelligent and knowledgeable - we were fascinated with one another. He had heard of Yeshua, and his crucifixion, but not the whole story - he hung on every word I uttered. These words went straight to his divine spark and overcame his conditioning. Surprising, given that in his world, women belonged in the home, lived in separate accommodation (if they could afford it) and the only legitimate reason to leave the house would be to attend the synagogue, but not with their husbands! Philo became a valuable member of our community; he was also our eyes and ears in Alexandria, and brought news from the outside world. If we were planning to start new communities we needed to be aware of what was going on in the outside world.

After the *The Secret Book of of John* I wrote *The Gospel of Thomas, The Gospel of Philip, the Hypostasis of the Archons, On the Origin of the World, The Exegesis of the Soul, The Book of Thomas the Contender, The Gospel of the Egyptians, Eugnostos the Blessed, The Sophia of Jesus Christ* and *The Dialogue of the Saviour*. Time does not permit me to summarise and explain my writings, so I have taken excerpts from some of them to give you a flavour of what I received from Yeshua. As your relationship with God is a personal experience, it is not for me to persuade you. If the time is right, you will have eyes to see and ears to hear...

THE GOSPEL OF MARY

Mary comforts the other disciples

*The disciples were in sorrow, shedding many tears, and saying,
"How are we to go among the unbelievers and announce the gospel of
our Kingdom of the Son of Man? They did not spare his life, so why
should they spare ours?"*

Then Mary arose, embraced them all, and began to speak to her brothers:

*"Do not remain in sorrow and doubt, for his Grace will guide you and
comfort you. Instead let us praise his greatness, for he has prepared us for
this. He is calling upon us to become fully human (Anthropos)".*

*Thus Mary turned their hearts towards the Good, and they began to
discuss the words of the Saviour.*

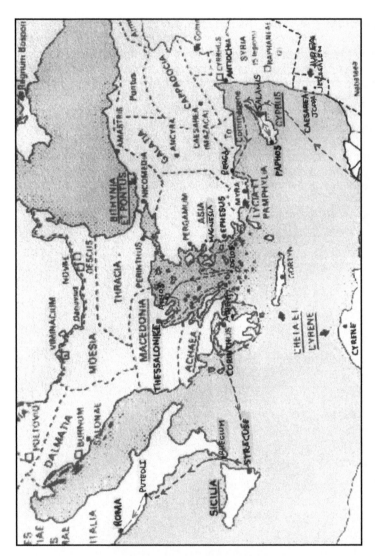

Figure 3: Map showing route taken by Mary Magdalene from Alexandria to Rome in 34 CE

CHAPTER VII

August 34 CE: Mary and the Apostles preach the Gospel

Yeshua came to me in a dream one night and said the writings were complete for now and it was time to reach out and preach the gospel according to the Way of the Heart. He told me to take Joseph of Arimathea, Lazarus, Peter, Paul, Andrew, Mark, the two Marys, Martha and Sarah of course. Sarah was almost a year old, curious about everything and anything! We would voyage to Rome and preach the gospel there, the capital of the world! We would stop in Cyprus, Turkey, Greek Macedonia, Greece, Sicily and finally Italy.

We would be away for months, so Luke, Bartholomew, James the son of Thaddaeus, Thomas and Matthias would sail up the Nile to preach the gospel and establish other communities in Egypt. James (son of Alphaeus), Matthew, Philip and Simon the Zealot stayed at Lake Mareotis.

To keep us safe, we would all carry holy water in a leather pouch and a wooden cross on our person, either around our necks or under our clothing. We would need to be vigilant - not all towns and cities would greet us warmly. Everything else, lodgings, food, drink, would be provided for. Of this I was confident - Yeshua would be with us every step of the way. I asked Peter to make wooden crosses for everyone in the community, some forty in number. This would be called the *crux quadrata*, or Greek cross, with four equal arms, recalling the crucifixion of Yeshua and the redeeming benefits of his Passion and death. The cross would become a sign both of Yeshua himself and of our faith. Making a sign of the cross would now be included in our prayers, dedications, benedictions and baptism ceremonies.

Salamis, Cyprus

When we arrived at the port in Alexandria, a ship was due to set sail to Salamis, Cyprus. Joseph arranged our passage with the captain and we set sail that same day. When we went ashore at Salamis, Paul and Peter preached the word of our Lord in the Jewish synagogue, and as us women were not permitted to enter, made our way to the market place to preach there. We attracted quite some attention; I was a single woman with child, who I nursed when she became unsettled. Otherwise she was minded by Mary Salome, who was always ready to take her off my hands! The women were particularly interested in what I had to say - many of them were mothers whose hearts had already been opened. Yeshua told me to heal bodies to awaken them, and then heal their hearts and souls. There was a young mother near the front whose young child was crying with all its might, its face bright red and contorted. I laid my hands on the child's head and prayed to Yeshua. The child instantly stopped and the mother looked at me with confusion and gratitude. She asked me to baptize her child, which I did there and then. And so the next day a larger crowd assembled and I read to them from the texts I had been writing for the last year. A middle-aged woman shouted out from the crowd,

"But how can we abandon our husbands and families? We cannot live on the word of God alone!"

"You do not have to, if you do not wish to", I replied. "All I am asking you to do is to follow your heart, for there you will find the treasure. We will help you set up groups and communities where you can worship or even live with your families according to the word of the Lord. All men and women are equal, we are all children of God in the eyes of the Lord. This is what Yeshua taught me!".

Paphos, Cyprus

After three days we journeyed to Paphos in the western part of Cyprus, where we met a man claiming to be a prophet, a Jew named Barjesus. He was with the deputy of the country, Sergius Paulus, a prudent man, who summoned Peter and Paul, as he wanted to hear the word of our Lord. But Barjesus the sorcerer tried to turn Sergius Paulus away from the faith. Paul turned to him and said,

"You enemy of all righteousness, will you not cease to pervert the right ways of the Lord? Behold, the hand of the Lord is upon you, and you shall be blind, not seeing the sun for a season."

Immediately a mist and a darkness fell on him, and the deputy believed - astonished at the doctrine of the Lord. We stayed with Sergius Paulus for a few days - he was truly insatiable for the words of the gospel! We made our excuses to leave and promised to return to help him set up communities in both Paphos and Salamis. We exchanged farewells as we had a long voyage ahead to Rome and many other places to visit on the way.

Perga, Turkey

Our next port of call was Perga in Pamphylia, Turkey, and the apostles went into the synagogue on the Sabbath day and sat down with the congregation. After the reading of the law by prophets and rulers of the synagogue, the apostles were invited to speak. Paul stood up and said,

"Men of Israel, listen to me! God according to his promise has raised unto Israel a Saviour, Yeshua, who sends the word of salvation. For those from Jerusalem, and their rulers, did not recognize him and condemned him to death. They could not find him guilty of any crime, because he was an innocent man, but Pilate ordered his crucifixion. And when this had been carried out, they took him down from the tree and laid him in a tomb. But our Father raised him from the dead, and he was seen from Galilee to Jerusalem many times.

So we share with you the good news, how that promise was made unto the fathers, in that Yeshua was raised up again, as it is also written in the second psalm, 'Thou art my Son, this day have I begotten thee'."

When the Jews left the synagogue, the Gentiles asked the apostles to return to preach on the following Sabbath, which they happily did. When the congregation left the synagogue, many of the Jews and new converts followed Paul and Peter, persuaded by their teachings to follow the Lord. Word spread amongst the locals and on the following Sabbath it seemed like the whole city came to hear the word of our Lord! But the Jews stirred up the devout women and the chief men of the city, and rallied around to form a mob who persecuted Paul and Peter, stripping them of their clothes and kicking them to the ground. But they were unharmed; they merely shook the dust from their clothes, laughing with joy as they left the city.

Magnesia ad Sipylum, Turkey

We travelled some distance onto Magnesia ad Sipylum, further north in Turkey. As we made our way towards the synagogue we were approached by a couple in great distress; as word had already travelled around the land of our preaching. They were carrying their child, limp in the father's arms, a daughter of around nine years or so.

"Please, please, can you heal our child?" the mother begged as she dropped to her knees.

The child was burning with a high fever, yet her face was drained of all colour and the parents feared she was near death. A crowd assembled, curious to see what would unfold. My heart opened as I looked at the mother, besieged by a look of powerless panic and desperation all over her face. As a mother myself, I knew how I would feel if anything happened to beloved Sarah. I prayed to Yeshua and the Father, took the leather pouch of holy water out of my pocket, removed the cork, and put it to her lips. You could hear a pin drop as the crowd looked on with bated breath. I was so happy when she opened her eyes and smiled at her father and mother, the colour suddenly restored to her face as the fever vanished! The crowd gasped in unison with a mixture of relief and surprise. The father threw himself prostrate on the ground and the mother embraced me crying out that they would never be able to thank me enough. I shook my head as I told them that I had not healed the child - it was the work of our gracious, loving Lord. I then proceeded to tell the now sizeable crowd about Yeshua. The words of Yeshua echoed in my ear, "Heal the bodies and then open their hearts..."

Delos, Greece

We left the following day once again pledging to return. Barnabus, the father of the sick girl, promised us an open house at any time and accompanied us to Smyrna on the coast where he arranged our passage to the Island of Delos. Located near the centre of the Cyclades archipelago in Greece, Delos had a position as a holy sanctuary for a millennium before Olympian Greek mythology made it the birthplace of Apollo and Artemis. As we approached the Sacred Harbour, three conical mounds stood out on the horizon, one named Mount Kynthos crowned with a sanctuary of Zeus. The local people were pagans and practised idolatry, worshipping Greek gods such as Dionysus and the Titaness Leto who, according to legend, was the mother of Apollo and Artemis.

We made our way to the main market square near the harbour, the Hellenistic Agora of the Competaliasts. In the centre of the square was a round marble monument dedicated to Hermes. In the northern portion of the square was an Ionic temple also dedicated to Hermes. There were many monuments, built by merchants, sea captains and bankers. The ground was paved with stones of gneiss and there were holes in the stones for the market stall tent poles.

There was no synagogue and so the apostles stayed with me while I preached in the agora about the wondrous life and teachings of Yeshua; how he was crucified although he had committed no crime, how he was raised from the dead and he truly is Christ. Some of them believed and wanted to learn more from Peter and Paul, along with many of the chief women, as it was rare to be preached to by a woman, and also a fair number of devout Greeks. A woman named Lydia, whose heart had been opened by the words of the Lord, asked what she could do to follow the Way. I baptized her and her family, and she said,

"If you have judged me to be faithful to the Lord, come to my house, and stay with me there."

I humbly replied that it was not for me to judge her and profusely expressed our gratitude as I thought to myself, just as Yeshua had said to me in my vision, everything would be provided.

As Yeshua had taught us, we prayed the Lord's Prayer with the assembled crowd. A young woman possessed of a spirit pushed her way to the front and cried out saying,

"These men are the servants of the most high God, which show us the way of salvation".

She did this continually for an hour or so, so Paul, turned and said to the spirit, "I command you in the name of Jesus Christ to come out of her." And the spirit left her immediately and she became quiet. But her masters were displeased, as the spirit had brought them a considerable income by fortune-telling - she was their cash cow. They seized Peter and Paul and escorted them before the rulers, and then to the magistrates saying,

"These men, being Jews, cause trouble in our city and teach customs which are not permitted according to Roman law"

This incited the crowds, as they were easily swayed and revelled in violence, and proceeded to tear off their clothes and beat them. When they tired of thrashing them, they threw them in prison, instructing the jailor to incarcerate them in the inner prison with their feet in stocks. At midnight Paul and Peter prayed, singing praises unto God, and the prisoners heard them. And suddenly there was a great earthquake, so that the foundations of the prison were shaken, all the doors were opened and all the prisoners' chains became undone and fell to the ground. The jailor awoke with the commotion. Seeing that the doors were open he assumed the prisoners had escaped and withdrew his sword ready to kill himself. But Peter cried out with a loud voice, saying,

"Do not harm yourself - we are all here!".

The jailor could not believe his ears and fell down at their feet, saying "Sirs, what must I do to be saved?"

They replied, "Believe in the Jesus Christ, and you and your family shall be saved."

And so Peter and Paul spoke with him and to all in his house the word of the Lord. The jailor bathed their wounds and invited them into his house, where he instructed his wife to prepare a meal for them all. He was so happy, believing in our Lord with all his heart!

The next day the jailor said to them, "The magistrates have ordered me to release you; so you are free men - go in peace."

"They have beaten us, Roman citizens, without trial" said Paul, "thrown us in prison and now they wish to throw us out? No, let them come themselves and release us!". The magistrates were fearful as it was illegal to beat Roman citizens without a trial, and immediately ordered them out of the city.

So without further ado they made their way to Lydia's house, where we were all staying and awaiting their return, having spent many hours extolling the virtues of our life at Lake Mareotis.

Once again we promised to return after our visit to Rome and made our way to the harbour as a ship was being loaded, due to set sail shortly for Thessaloniki, Greek Macedonia.

Athos Greece

There was a stiff southerly breeze filling our sails, giving us a speed of around six knots or so. The captain was happy with our progress - it was some 280 miles to Thessaloniki and he was keen to return to his family who he had been parted from for some months. But when we awoke the following day the skies had darkened, the sea had turned grey and the waves looked confused, making our ship pitch violently in between the peaks and troughs. The captain went quiet. He clutched the wheel, peering into the distance with a furrowed brow. In hindsight, we should have found shelter on the mainland, but we kept going - the captain was trying to ride out the storm. I clutched Sarah to me and silently prayed to Yeshua.

The wind had veered round to a north westerly and we could not make our course to Thessaloniki. The captain looked even more worried...he said we had been blown off course and had no choice but to make for Athos, home to Mount Athos, located in north eastern Greece. In Greek mythology, Athos is the name of one of the giants that challenged the Greek gods. Athos threw a massive rock against Poseidon which fell in the Aegean sea and became Mount Athos. The captain told us that the seas surrounding the peninsula were highly dangerous. Greek history recorded two fleet disasters; in 492 BC Darius, the king of Persia lost 300 ships carrying 20,000 men, and in 411 BC the Spartans lost a fleet of 50 ships. These disastrous tales of shipwrecks did nothing to allay our fears!

The captain sensed we were near land and instructed the crew to sound in order to measure the depth of water under the keel. It was twenty fathoms; when we had gone a little further, they sounded again and was now fifteen fathoms. Then, fearing we would be blown onto the rocks, the crew lowered all the sails and dropped four anchors out of the stern to stop the ship and awaited daylight. It was a long starless night and I prayed thanks to our Lord when the sun appeared above the horizon. The storm had abated, but we still had strong headwinds which prevented us from entering the port of Klement, and we anchored as close to the shore as the captain dared. The seamen lowered the tender to the leeward side and helped us on board. We could now see the majestic Mount Athos, towering above us in such a regal manner! The captain rowed us into the harbour where the water was quiet and still. As we walked ashore, Mother Mary was so overwhelmed by the wonderful and wild natural beauty of the mountain that she asked her son Yeshua to bless it and make it her garden. A voice was heard saying,

"Let this place be your inheritance and your garden, a paradise and a haven of salvation for those seeking to be saved."

From that moment the mountain was consecrated as the garden of the Mother of our Lord and was out of bounds to all other women. All of us had heard the voice and the captain and his crew threw themselves prostrate on the ground. With a look of bewilderment, the captain asked what they could do to be saved.

"Just believe in Jesus Christ with all your heart!" I replied, smiling at them.

I baptized them there and then with my holy water. There were a few onlookers who followed us as we walked to the market square. A small crowd assembled as I preached the gospel. Peter had a vision that night instructing him to stay here and start a Christian community. Andrew, his brother, volunteered to stay and help him. We would return to collect them on our way home from Rome. The community would later be known as *Simonopetra Monastery*.

My work was done here, for now at least, as Athos was in good hands with two of Yeshua's disciples. The captain was keen to return to his ship - he was understandably anxious having left his ship at anchor open to the elements in such dangerous waters.

Thessaloniki, Greek Macedonia

We weighed anchor and set sail for Thessaloniki, capital of Greek Macedonia some 75 miles to the west. Founded in 315 BCE by King Cassander of Macedon, the city was named after the half-sister of Alexander the Great. It was an important city, linking Rome and Byzantium - the great centres of commerce.

The Marys and I made our way to the market square, as Paul and the others entered the synagogue, where they preached for the next three Sabbaths. Many of the Greeks believed, and some of the Jews, including Jason, who invited us to stay with him in his house. Jason was from Tarsus in Syria, the same city as Paul, and so they reminisced and happily shared stories about their homeland.

But the Jews who did not believe became enraged with envy, and gathered an unruly crowd who whipped the city into uproar, and vandalized Jason's house. They brought Jason and the apostles before the rulers of the city crying,

"These men have turned the world upside down are here before you, hosted by Jason. They contravene the decrees of Caesar, saying there is another king, one 'Yeshua'."

And so Jason was arrested. Although it was dark, the others were ordered to leave the city and made their way to Berea, a neighbouring city. They found shelter in the synagogue, and after Jason was released the following day we joined them in Berea. The people there were much more gracious and welcoming than those of Thessaloniki, in that they received the word with open minds, and studied the scriptures daily in an attempt to verify our words.

There was a certain man at Berea, who was a cripple from birth who heard Paul speak. Paul could see that he had faith to be healed, and said with a loud voice, "Stand upright on your feet!." And the man got up and walked, with elation in his face for all to behold. When the people saw what Paul had done, they announced,

"The gods are come down to us in the likeness of men." And the priest of Jupiter, who happened to be in the city, brought oxen and garlands to the gates preparing to sacrifice them. And when the apostles heard of this, they ran among the people crying out,

"Sirs, why do you do these things? We are ordinary men like you, and preach that you should turn from these sacrificial offerings towards our Father, who made heaven, earth and sea, and all living things; who in times past suffered all nations to walk in their own ways. Nevertheless, he gave us rain from heaven, and fruitful seasons, filling our hearts with food and gladness."

So on this occasion at least, they persuaded the people from making sacrifices. But when the Jews of Thessaloniki learned the word of the Lord was preached and well received at Berea, they came along and stirred up the people. We decided to leave before the crowd got too heated! We were sent on our way; this time we set sail for Athens.

Athens, Greece

When we arrived in Athens, it seemed like the whole city was worshiping idols! So the apostles disputed earnestly in the synagogue with the Jews, and with the devout persons, and us women preached in the marketplace. Certain philosophers of the Epicurean and Stoic schools enquired of our teaching, saying, "They seem to speak of strange gods", because we preached to them about Yeshua and the resurrection. They suggested the apostles accompany them to Aeropagus, the great rock near the Acropolis, a popular meeting place. Here the philosophers asked,

"May we know what this new doctrine is? For you bring strange ideas to our ears: we wish to know the meaning of these things."

Then Paul stood in the midst of Mars' Hill, and said,

"Men of Athens, I see that in all matters you are too superstitious. For on my way here, I found an altar with this inscription: TO THE UNKNOWN GOD. But God who made the world and all things therein, seeing that he is Lord of heaven and earth, does not dwell in temples made with hands, for in him we live and move, as certain of your poets have said, 'for we are also his offspring.' Since we are the offspring of God, we ought not to think that the Godhead is like gold, or silver, or stone, graven by art or man-made."

And when they heard of the resurrection, some laughed in disbelief, but others were intrigued and sincerely asked questions.

Corinth, Grecee

We sailed from Athens to Corinth, and met a Jew called Aquila, who came from Pontus. He and his wife Priscilla had recently arrived from Italy because Claudius had ordered all Jews to leave Rome. Aquila, a tentmaker by trade, invited us to stay with him and his family. Paul preached to the Jews in the synagogue that Yeshua was Christ. But the Jews jeered and cursed Paul, accusing him of blasphemy. So Paul said,

"Your blood be upon your own heads; I am clean, and will now go to see the Gentiles."

So they left immediately and knocked on the door of the adjoining house which belonged to Justus, a believer, who invited them to stay with him and his family.

Then our Lord spoke to me in the night by a vision, "Do not be afraid, speak up, for I am with you, and you will be safe in this city as I have many followers here."

Crispus, who was the chief ruler of the synagogue, believed in the Lord with all his heart, and so many of the Corinthians also believed and asked to be baptized. We were approached by an Alexandrian Jew named Apollos, an eloquent man well versed with the scriptures. He was instructed in the way of the Lord, but knew only the baptism of John. When Aquila and Priscilla heard him speaking boldly in the synagogue, they took him aside afterwards to share with him what they had learned from our teachings.

I said to Apollos and the other believers, "Have you received the Holy Spirit since you came to Christ?"

And they replied, "We haven't even *heard* of the Holy Spirit!"

And so I baptized them in the name of Yeshua. And when I laid my hands on them, they spoke in tongues, and prophesied. Aquila and Priscilla quietly suggested that Apollos and some of the others be made disciples, as they had convinced many Jews and Greeks that Yeshua was Christ.

The men were twelve in number and the apostles separated them, sending them to foreign lands so that in the space of the next two years, all Jews and Greeks who lived in Asia would hear the word of Lord Yeshua. And our Lord performed many miracles through the disciples. The name of Yeshua was magnified and became well known. Consequently the number of believers grew rapidly.

Syracuse, Sicily

On the penultimate leg of our journey, we joined a ship bound for Syracuse in Sicily, a considerable distance of at least 400 miles - and this was if the wind allowed us to sail there directly on one tack, which was highly unlikely!

Joseph looked worried. He was concerned about the seaworthiness of the vessel and spoke with both the owner and captain of the ship,

"Sirs, I am concerned about the safety of this voyage; not only with the stowing of the ship's stores but also with its sea worthiness!".

But they ignored him, and we set sail as a south wind blew softly. But not long after, a tempestuous wind arose, called the *euroclydon*, a cyclonic north easterly wind which blows in the Mediterranean in autumn and winter. There was no way we could circumvent the storm, and we soon faced a gale on the nose. We could not bear up into the wind and the captain had no choice other than to let the ship bear away.

We were violently tossed by the tempest, so the next day the captain ordered some of the ships stores to be thrown overboard to lighten the load. By the third day it was 'all hands on deck' as we continued to be battered by the storm and the crew were all but exhausted! Thunderous dark grey clouds and driving rain prevented us from seeing neither sun nor stars for many days, and we began to lose all hope of survival!

That night, an angel of our Lord appeared and said, "Fear not, Mary, you and all that sail with you will be saved - you will find shelter on a certain island."

After fourteen nights the crew sensed that we were near land, dropped four anchors out of the stern, and awaited dawn. As the crew were about to abandon ship, I implored them all to eat saying,

"This is the fourteenth day you have fasted; I pray you take some meat for the sake of your health, for not a hair shall fall from any of your heads!"

I asked them all to assemble, took bread and broke it, gave thanks to our Lord and we began to eat. We also ate some meat and the general mood cheered considerably! When we had all eaten enough, they lightened the ship even more, throwing the rest of the grain sacks overboard. When we awoke the following morning we were relieved to see the storm had finally abated and we were within sight of land. The captain recognised this as Syracuse, our original destination! He ordered the crew to hoist the mainsail, weigh anchor and sail towards the harbour. We prayed thanks to our Lord and were most grateful to set on dry land. The ship was no longer seaworthy and badly in need of repair, but we were all safe and sound as the angel had promised.

Syracuse was founded around 730 BC by Greek settlers from Corinth and Tenea. Famous for being the birthplace of the mathematician and engineer Archimedes, born in 287 BCE, he was considered the greatest mathematician of antiquity. Described by Cicero as "the greatest Greek city and the most beautiful of them all", it equalled Athens in size during the fifth century BC and was the most important city in Magna Graecia.

The women and I made our way to the market square and the apostles went in search of the synagogue. It happened to be the Sabbath day and Paul was invited to preach the word of the Lord. He was well received on this occasion and the chief man of the island whose name was Publius, invited us to stay with him to recover from our nearly disastrous voyage. We were well looked after and felt restored after three days. While we were there, Publius' father became very sick with a fever and bloody flux. I entered his bedroom, prayed to Yeshua, laid hands on him, and healed him. News spread over the island and others came to be healed, successfully! When it was time to leave we were furnished with many provisions for our ongoing voyage.

Puteoli, Campania, Italy

We joined a ship from Alexandria, which had sheltered in Melita and whose sign was Castor and Pollux. We crossed the strait of Messina and came to Rhegium on the mainland of Italy. We waited less than a day for a southerly wind to blow us north and we arrived the next day in Puteoli, where the local people invited us to stay for a few days to hear the word of the Lord.

It obtained the name of *Puteoli* from the stench arising from the sulphur springs in its neighbourhood. This is because Puteoli lies in the centre of *Campi Flegrei*, a caldera. The town became important as a result of its excellent natural harbour, which was protected by a mole and extended for two miles as far as the neighbouring resort of Baiae. Puteoli was the great emporium for the Alexandrian grain ships, and the main hub for goods exported from Campania, including blown glass, mosaics, wrought iron, and marble.

The Roman naval base at nearby Misenum housed the largest naval fleet in the ancient world. The local volcanic sand, *pozzolana*, formed the basis for the first effective concrete, as it reacts chemically with water. Instead of just evaporating off slowly, the water would turn this sand and lime mix into a mortar strong enough to bind lumps of aggregate into a load bearing-unit. This made possible the building of the cupola of Pantheon, the first real dome.

Rome, Italy

From here we journeyed on foot along the Appian Way to Rome, a distance of some 170 miles. Sarah for one was delighted to be no longer at sea! The men happily took it in turns to carry her on their shoulders, as her joy and enthusiasm for everything she saw was most infectious! Almost everything seemed a miracle to her! When the local people heard of us, they came to meet us as far as Forum Appi, a post station some 43 miles southeast of Rome. Incredulous at the distance we had travelled and charmed by young bubbly Sarah, they were most hospitable. They warned us of the unscrupulous boatmen and innkeepers and arranged lodgings for us, eager to hear about the Lord Jesus Christ. We were greatly heartened by this and joyfully gave thanks to our Lord. The following day we were met at the Three Taverns, on the Appian Way, designed for the reception of travellers. This would be our final resting place as we were some 30 miles or so from Rome. We were quite some gathering by now!

We all made our way to the market square, as the Jews had been expelled from the city and there were no synagogues for the apostles to preach in. I remembered Yeshua's words; first heal the body and the heart will follow - truly the crowds multiplied and many believed and wished to be baptized.

News travels fast and word reached the Roman Emperor, Tiberius Caesar, of our arrival. An invitation was sent to us to join him for dinner. We had been advised by the centurion bearing the invitation that it was customary for those visiting the Emperor to take him a gift and I wondered what I should take. Once again, that night an angel came to me in a dream saying I should take an egg! I was puzzled somewhat by this, being an unusual gift, but trusted whatever messages I received from my beloved.

I was honoured to be sat next to the Emperor and waited until the main course to rebuke Caesar for the crucifixion of Yeshua, carried out by his governor in Judea, Pontius Pilate. I handed him the egg - a symbol of new life - saying, "Christ is risen!".

Caesar looked puzzled at both my gift and accompanying comment. As he took the egg he replied,

"How could anyone rise from the dead? It is as impossible as it would be for that egg to change from white to red!"

As he uttered these words the egg in his hand turned blood red! The look on his face was a sight to behold! I tried to contain my own surprise and keep a straight face! I watched the astonishment on his face quickly turn to anger and sadness, as he realized what a travesty of justice had been carried out by his governor, Pontius Pilate. The murder of an innocent man, no ordinary man, possibly the son of God! He sat there speechless, shaking his head in utter dismay. His demeanour was sober for the rest of the evening and as we got up to leave he expressed his sincere regret for the actions of his officials.

He went on to say that as Jews were now officially *persona non grata*, and he could not personally guarantee our safety, regretfully it would be prudent for us to leave and avoid possible injury to ourselves. He thanked us for going to such lengths to visit him and grant him a personal audience..

We heard later that Caesar had Pontius Pilate removed as governor of Judea and sent to Gaul in exile.

We left Rome on the following day to begin our long journey home to Alexandria, glad of heart. We retraced our steps, voyaging on the trading ships, but thankfully this time without storms! We preached along the way, and were warmly greeted by our new friends - truly happy to see us safe and well!

We were reunited with Peter and Andrew in Athos and arrived back in Alexandria in January 35 CE, some five months after we had left.

THE GOSPEL OF MARY

Peter asks Mary to teach

Peter said to Mary: "Sister, we know that the Teacher loved you differently from other women. Tell us whatever you remember of any words he told you which we have not yet heard."

Mary said to them: "I will speak to you of that which has not been given to you to hear. I had a vision of the Teacher and I said to him:-

"Lord I see you now in this vision." And he answered,

'You are blessed, for the sight of me does not disturb you. There where is the nous lies the treasure.'

Then I said to him: 'Lord, when someone meets you in a moment of vision, is it through the soul (psyche) that they see, or is it through the Spirit (Pneuma)?'

The teacher answered,
'It is neither through the soul nor the spirit, but the nous between the two which see the vision, and is this which (....)"*

CHAPTER VIII

January 35 CE: Home again

It was simply wonderful to be home again, reunited with everyone, back at Lake Mareotis!

Bartholomew, James, Thaddaeus, Thomas, Matthias and Luke were back from Egypt having set up communities in three of the thirteen nomes in Egypt. One near Faiyum, Nag Hammadi and Oxyrynchus, all similar to Lake Mareotis. Simple in structure, near a living water source, and somewhere quiet.

There was a great reunion amongst the apostles and many tales recounted around our evening repast. We had covered many miles and met many people, not all welcoming! And they all made such a fuss of Sarah, 16 months old now and changed so much in just five months; starting to talk, well, giving instructions mostly! She had all the men wrapped around her little finger, and she knew it! She would ask for something and just stare imploringly up at them with her mesmerizing blue eyes and their resolve simply melted! Mary Salome and I were more resilient to her methods so she didn't waste her time asking us if one of the men were around, which they invariably were! 'No' was not the answer she was looking for! She was enjoying her new found freedom, waddling around now, shrieking with delight at every small thing, happy as the day was long. She was such a blessing and brought so much joy to each and every one of us - I thanked God every day!

Philip was particularly excited about our return, or more specifically, Sarah's, and was most anxious to show her something. He had been busy in our absence, making toys for her! He pointed to a palm tree close to the hall where he had made a swing out of wood and suspended it with rope. Sarah leapt to her feet with excitement and rushed over to try it out. Laughter rang out from them both as Philip pushed her, higher and higher. She could not get enough of this new past time! Luckily, there would be no shortage of volunteers - joy is so infectious and there was more than enough pleasure for both parties!

Then Philip announced he had something else to show her - he couldn't wait to show us all his 'piece de resistance'. Sarah was reluctantly lifted out of the swing and led by Philip into the kitchen. There stood a gleaming chestnut rocking horse! Sarah gasped and stood there rooted to the spot, open mouthed for a few seconds before raising her arms in great excitement, waiting to be raised astride her new steed. She was a little young for it and had to be held in place, but she loved it so much! Philip beamed with pride - she was a very lucky girl indeed. She would spend many hours on her beloved horse; she called him *Lucky*, going on imaginary treks into the desert and beyond, chatting excitedly to her four-legged friend about everything and anything!

It was astounding that not a hair on the head of any of us had been harmed... except we were protected, and would be as long as we remained on earth and served our Lord. Light attracts dark, so there would always be challenges, but nothing we could not overcome - we would never be abandoned to the forces of evil.

It was quite some celebration the first Sabbath after our return. Peter led the ceremony, recounting his experiences at Athos, Mother Mary's garden. We sang that night with such intensity and elation I thought my heart would burst! If someone told me this was heaven on earth I would have believed them!

And when sunrise came, we solemnly prayed with our arms raised to the heavens, then returned quietly to our cabins, to resume studying and writing. I put Sarah down for a nap and was able to write for two to three hours at that time. When she awoke, Mary Salome would swoop in and take her for a snack and play with her all day long - I am not sure who enjoyed it more!

Peter, Paul, Andrew and Mark were keen to revisit all the places we had promised to return to, which they duly made plans to do. And so within the next two years eleven communities were founded in Asia Minor and Europe; not including Lake Mareotis. There would be twelve in total, as in the twelve apostles.

Luke and Mark sailed directly to Salamis in Cyprus and with the help of Sergius Paulus, founded communities at Salamis and Paphos.

Paul was accompanied by Bartholomew and sailed to Syria where they founded communities at Tyre and Antioch.

Simon Peter and Andrew travelled to Turkey and then Greece. They founded communities at Perga, Pamphylia and Magnesia ad Sipylum in Turkey. They sailed onto the island of Delos in Greece and finally Athos, where we had been close to being shipwrecked, and where Peter had had a vision to start a community.

The apostles visited regularly and their numbers swelled to around a thousand in all. Here at Lake Mareotis our numbers were up to one hundred and fifty!

Philo continued to visit regularly, whose company I much enjoyed. I was pleasantly surprised when he asked me to baptize him, and yet not, for it was not me - it was through Yeshua touching his heart. I will never forget the look on his face - a look of humility I had rarely witnessed in this erudite man. His heart had finally got the better of his huge brain - not before time! We cannot learn about God through philosophy; faith is not an intellectual pursuit, it is only in surrendering that we can open our hearts. This can be pretty scary, as the mind prefers to be in control.

I needed to think about Sarah's education - she was barely three years old but so keen to learn, and in my eyes she was ready. I asked Philo if he would be her tutor and tears filled his eyes - he had no children and was very fond of her. He said he had no experience of working with such young children, but was happy to see how they got on. I was sure he would be guided - his heart was certainly in it!

I would have to ask Mary Salome's permission of course! She considered herself number one charge to Sarah! Mary Salome was an intelligent woman and she recognized Philo's intellectual training - she wanted the very best for Sarah, as I did. She said with a wry smile that she found it easier being in the outdoors with Sarah to the copying of my texts, but she would do whatever was required of her. She was devoted to me, Sarah and the Lord - I was very blessed with the people I had around me.

Philo brought books from Alexandria and would stay for two months or so at a time before returning to the city to tend to his affairs. Sarah would leap up and down with excitement when she saw him arriving, and cling to his legs when he had to leave for to the city! There were continual uprisings between the Greeks and the Jews, and the Romans invariably sought his counsel or intervention. The Roman emperor Caligula was creating problems, trying to install statues of the Roman gods in the great synagogue, which the Jewish council, the Sanhedrin, had succeeded in resisting so far.

Philo said he was happy with us. He had everything materially but was spiritually starved in the city, here we were poor but had everything and more!

Philo started Sarah with the Hebrew alphabet, as that was my native tongue, and in a year or two, would move onto the Greek alphabet. We lived in a Greek speaking city, and all my writings were in Greek, so it was essential she could understand those. Philo said Sarah was highly intelligent, which every mother likes to hear of course, and spending so much time in a one-to-one with Philo made her progress swift and seemingly effortless. There were never any tears, just gales of laughter from them both. Philo learnt to stop before she got tired, either for rest or nourishment, so she was always eager to get back to their play-studies. It must have been hard for Mary Salome in the beginning. She never said anything, but I saw it in her face that she missed Sarah. I prayed for her, and reminded her that Philo would not be with us forever - even little Sarah seemed to sense this and never wasted a moment with him.

All Sarah's lessons were outside, unless it was the middle of the day and they could find no shade, which was rare as we were surrounded by towering palm trees and a gentle breeze from the Mediterranean, making the temperature perfect.

Philo taught her simple arithmetic by counting pebbles by the shore. Everything was a game, and she grasped new concepts quickly. Philo confided in me that he had found his true vocation - if someone had foretold this he would never have believed it in a hundred years! He looked so happy, and at least ten years younger!

I wish I had had a teacher like Philo; sharp intellect combined with endless patience, and the magic ingredient of love was highly potent. His young pupil never seemed to tire of him. It was a joy to behold, and I thanked Yeshua every day for bringing him into our lives. He said Sarah was like a sponge, but never full, insatiable for knowledge.

He pointed out the stars and the planets, explaining how we were all affected by their position in the sky, which was continually changing. From the moment we are born until the day we die and become dust - everything is a cycle. Even the vast oceans were affected by the waxing and waning of the moon!

I heard him explaining to Sarah one day that Plato had written that we all had our very own birth star! It became a bedtime ritual - staring into the star lit sky wondering which one was theirs. Philo said that he was sure they came from the same constellation because they got on so well.

He never spoke down to her and treated her as an equal; her whole being seemed to grow visibly on a daily basis. We were so blessed to have Philo with us. Such happy days indeed! Sarah would leap out of the bed in the mornings and lay her head down at night with a beatific smile on her face.

But nothing lasts forever...

THE GOSPEL OF MARY

Mary describes the ascent of the soul

"I left the world with the aid of another world; a design was erased, by virtue of a higher design. Henceforth I travel toward Repose, where time rests in the Eternity of time; I go now into Silence."

Having said all this, Mary became silent, for it was in silence that the Teacher spoke to her. Then Andrew began to speak, and said to his brothers:

"Tell me, what do you think of these things she has been telling us? As for me, I do not believe that the Teacher would speak like this. These ideas are too different from those we have known." And Peter added: "How is it possible that the Teacher talked in this manner with a woman about secrets of which ourselves are ignorant? Must we change our customs, and listen to this woman? Did he really choose her, and prefer her to us?"

Then Mary wept, and answered him: "My brother Peter, what can you be thinking? Do you believe that is just my own imagination, that I invented this vision? Or do you believe that I would lie about our Teacher?"

At this, Levi spoke up,

"Peter, you have always been hot-tempered, and now we see you repudiating a woman, just as our adversaries do. Yet if the Teacher held her worthy, who are you to reject her? Surely the Teacher knew her very well, for he loved her more than us. Therefore let us atone, and become fully human (Anthropos), so that the Teacher can take root in us. Let us grow as demanded of us, and walk forth to spread the gospel, without trying to lay down any rules and laws other than those he witnessed."

When Levi had said these words, they all went forth to spread the gospel.

CHAPTER IX

July 38 CE: Anti-Jewish violence and James' martyrdom

Tiberius, the emperor I had dined with in Rome, died in 37 CE and was succeeded by Herod Agrippa's friend Caligula. Herod Agrippa had previously been overheard expressing a wish for Tiberius' death and the advancement of Caligula, for which he had been put in prison. When Caligula came to power, Herod Agrippa was promptly released and made king of a section of Palestine. Agrippa was awarded the *ornamenta praetoria* and could use the title *amicus caesaris* ('friend of Caesar'). Caligula also presented him with a gold chain equal in weight to the iron one he had worn in prison, which Agrippa later dedicated to the Temple of Jerusalem on his return to his ancestral homeland. He governed Judea to the satisfaction of the Jews. He displayed great zeal, in both private and public, for Judaism.

Because of his Jewish sympathies, his passage through Alexandria in 38 CE instigated anti-Jewish riots. He was on his way from Rome to take his throne in the Jewish homeland. He had waited until summer, to take advantage of Etesian winds by sailing to Palestine via Alexandria. He was known to Philo, having borrowed large sums of money from Philo's brother, Alexander, and would stay in Philo's private home.

Philo had advised Agrippa to make an inconspicuous entrance given the fragility of relations between the Greeks and the Jews. But Agrippa ignored this prudent advice and his arrival was announced by the accompaniment of a bodyguard of spearmen, decked in armour overlaid with gold and silver. The Jews had successfully courted Roman favour, and now felt the brunt of Alexandrian hostility, particularly by the Greek community. A series of outrages ensued, which Flaccus, the governor of Alexandria made no attempt to stop. The unemployed mob gathered in the gymnasium, openly venting hostility towards Agrippa. Even worse, they ridiculed him. They found Carabas, the poor lunatic who lived on the streets, decked him out in royal regalia, and hailed him loudly with the Aramaic for 'Lord'.

A mob met in the theatre and demanded that images of Caligula be placed in the synagogues. There were burnings, lootings and razings. The objection was that the Jews should not get away with not paying divine honours to the emperor. The Jews were prepared to make offerings *on behalf* of the emperor but not directly to him. The former they would do, the latter they refused on the grounds of idolatry.

As a final insult, the mob dragged an old statue of a charioteer from the gymnasium and set it up in the Great Synagogue. Flaccus once again failed to intervene and incited further violence by making a public proclamation questioning the Jews' position in Alexandria and denouncing them as 'foreigners and aliens'. The mob interpreted this as giving them free reign. They evicted the Jews from the four other quarters of the city and crowded them into a small part of Delta. They pillaged the now empty houses and workshops and prevented the Jewish tradespeople from carrying on their work. Those who desperately sought food in the marketplace were seized, stabbed, dragged along the streets and trampled on. Others were stoned and their property burned.

Flaccus arrested thirty-eight members of the Jewish senate and had them scourged in the theatre, some to the point of death. To add insult to injury, scourging was reserved for commoners rather than the Alexandrians. Some of the Jews who were scourged were crucified. Flaccus carried out a search for arms in the Jewish homes, but found none.

The governor's attempts to ingratiate himself with Caligula failed completely. A centurion was sent from Italy to catch him off guard. The Jews should have been celebrating their great autumn festival, the feast of Tabernacles, but festivities had been cancelled because the Jews were still in mourning and many of their leaders imprisoned or dead. But the Jews interpreted it as a sign of their vindication and it prompted a spontaneous celebration. Flaccus was taken to Rome and banished to a desolate island in the Aegean Sea. Caligula ordered his execution shortly after.

In 39 CE, the Greeks and the Jews sent delegations to Rome to intercede with the emperor himself. The Greeks were led by Apion, a staunch opponent of the Jews, and Philo led the Jewish contingent. On their arrival in Rome, Caligula was distracted and more interested in his desire to be worshipped as the incarnation of Zeus.

When Caligula finally granted an audience to the two delegations, the Jews were unnerved by the Emperor's opening remark,

"Are you the god-haters who do not believe me to be a god, a god acknowledged among all the other nations but not to be named by you?".

The discussions never went deeper than a superficial level, and the two delegations returned to Alexandria having resolved nothing.

In 40 CE, at the risk of his own life, or at least of his liberty, Herod Agrippa interceded with Caligula on behalf of the Jews - Caligula was attempting to set up his statue in the Temple at Jerusalem. Agrippa's efforts were successful and he persuaded Caligula to rescind this order thus preventing the Temple's desecration. However, Caligula issued a second order to have his statue erected in the Temple. Another statue of himself, of colossal size, was built of gilt brass. The Temple of Jerusalem was then transformed into a temple for Caligula, and it was called the *Temple of Illustrious Gaius the New Jupiter.*

In January 41 CE Caligula was assassinated and succeeded by his uncle Claudius. When the news reached Alexandria around a month later, fresh violence erupted. The Jews, humiliated under his rule and grievously abused by the Alexandrians, armed themselves and enlisted support from fighters from Syria and other parts of Egypt.

Before news of this reached Claudius he had been impressed with his Jewish friends, Herod Agrippa and his brother Herod of Chalcis, with how they addressed the grievances of the Alexandrian Jews. Claudius reinstated the Jews' former rights and privileges, taken away by the folly and madness of Caligula. His only condition was that hostilities between the two parties would cease after posting his edict.

A few months later, the Alexandrian citizen body sent further delegations to Rome to congratulate Claudius on his accession. Philo represented the Jews, and Dionysius, a Greek nationalist known for his anti-Jewish policy, represented the Greeks. In November 41 CE, Claudius wrote a carefully composed letter addressed to both the Greeks and the Jews. He refused to judge which party was responsible for the initial riots, but demanded that the hostilities end. He confirmed the Greeks as the true Alexandrians, but demanded tolerance towards the Jews. Claudius answered the question about the highly desired citizenship for Jews in Alexandria - it never existed for the majority. The Jews were what they had always been - a race living with certain privileges in a city *'not their own'.* Claudius also demanded the end of any future uprisings, with or without the help of Jews from other lands, or his benevolence towards them would cease.

Philo was now in his sixties and this would be his last political stand - in his opinion it was not a wholly undesirable outcome, and he wished to step back from political life in Alexandria. He was tired of years of trying to quell disturbances in the city. Furthermore, his heart was elsewhere - he wanted to return to Lake Mareotis and focus on his tutoring.

Philo relayed this to me on his return to Lake Mareotis and was confident we were safe, at least as long as Claudius was emperor in Rome.

The apostles were spreading their wings and preaching the gospel far and wide. James, son of Zebedee, brother of John, preached throughout Judea and Samaria and in 40 CE travelled to Spain to spread the word there. However, he felt he had made little headway, gaining just nine disciples, so he returned to Judea.

While he was preaching in Judea, a magician named Hermogenes, who was allied with the Pharisees, sent one of his followers named Philetus to James. Philetus was instructed to confront the apostle and convince him, in the presence of the Jews, that his preaching was false. But James showed Philetus that he preached the truth, and performed many miracles for all to see. Philetus returned to Hermogenes saying he intended to become a disciple of James and urged Hermogenes to do likewise.

Hermogenes was furious. By his magical skills he made Philetus immobile and cried,

"Now we shall see whether your James can release you!"

Philetus sent word of this to James by his servant, and James sent him his handkerchief, saying,

"Have him hold this cloth and say, 'The Lord upholds all who are falling; he sets the prisoners free'."

As soon as Philetus touched the handkerchief he was freed of his invisible bonds, mocked Hermogenes' magical arts, and hastened to join James.

Hermogenes' anger knew no bounds. He summoned the demons and demanded they bring James to him in chains, along with Philetus, to discourage his other followers from challenging him. The demons swarmed in the air around James and began to howl, saying,

"Apostle James, have mercy on us, for we are already on fire before our time has come!"

"For what purpose have you come to me?" asked James.

They answered, "Hermogenes sent us to bring you and Philetus to him, but as soon as we reached you, an angel of God bound us with fiery chains and tormented us sorely!"

James replied, "Let the angel of God release you, and go back to Hermogenes and bring him to me, bound but unharmed!"

So off they went, seized Hermogenes, tied his hands around his back, and brought him to James saying to their captive, "You sent us, and where we went we were burned and sorely tormented!"

To James the demons begged, "Give us power over him, so that we can get revenge for the wrongs he has done you and our own fiery torments!"

James said to them, "Here is Philetus standing before you! Why don't you lay hold of him?"

They answered contritely, "We cannot lay a finger on as much as an ant, as long as it is in your house!"

James said calmly to Philetus, "Let us return good for evil, as Christ taught us to do. Hermogenes put you in bonds, now you unbind him!".

His bindings fell to the ground and James turned to him, "You are free, it is not in our faith to convert anyone against his or her will!"

The magician cried, "I know the anger of the demons! They will kill me unless you give me something to keep me safe!"

James nodded in agreement and gave him his staff, and Hermogenes brought all his books about magic to be burnt. But James, fearing the smoke from the fire might do harm to those unaware of the danger, ordered him to throw them into the sea. He duly did, and returned to James, prostrated himself and clinging to his feet, crying,

"You have borne with me while I envied and sought to do you harm! Please receive me now as a penitent?"

Thereafter he began to live perfectly as Yeshua taught us, so much so that many miracles took place through him.

The Jews were indignant at seeing Hermogenes convert to following Christ, but James preached the gospel and many of them believed. Abiathar, the high priest, incited an uprising amongst the people, then put a rope around the apostle's neck and brought him to Herod Agrippa. Agrippa was envious of James' power and popularity and resented the notion that any man other than himself could be called divine. He ordered him to be beheaded. He was keen to crush this dangerous movement before it gathered momentum.

As James was led away there lay a paralyzed man by the side of the road who called out to James, begging him to cure him. James turned to him and said,

"In the name of Jesus Christ, for whose faith I am led to execution, stand up and bless your saviour!".

The man stood up, and with tears of joy rolling down his face, blessed the Lord. The scribe, named Josiah, who had put the rope round James' neck, knelt at his feet, begged his pardon, and asked to be made a Christian. Observing this, Abiathar had him seized and shouted,

"Unless you curse the name of Christ, you will be beheaded with James!", to which Josiah replied,

"Cursed be you and all your days, and blessed be the name of Jesus Christ forever!"

Abiathar had him punched in the mouth and sent a messenger to Herod Agrippa to obtain an order for his beheading. While the two awaited their execution, James asked for a jug of water and he baptized Josiah. Both of them had their heads struck off and achieved martyrdom.

James was beheaded on 25th March 43 CE, the feast of the Lord's annunciation, and was transferred to Compostela on 25th July. It took five months to build his tomb and he was buried on 30th December.

James' execution sent shock waves through the Christian community. Bad news travels fast, even reaching his brother John, who at that time was preaching in Asia Minor. John sent word that he was returning to Judea to pay his respects and that his brother's body should not be transferred to Spain before his arrival.

Grief can do strange things to a man's mind. John was a good man, but his torment developed into a blind rage and he blamed me. He had never approved of me leading the apostles and being 'head' of a community. As far as he was concerned, I was directly responsible for his brother's death and he was looking for revenge.

Immediately after paying his respects, he requested an audience with King Herod Agrippa. He told Herod Agrippa that he had to make a stand, to show no weakness, and to seek out the root of the problem. I was the problem and Herod Agrippa should have me arrested. I am not sure if he wanted me executed, or just imprisoned, but we had left before the Roman soldiers arrived.

Seeing how James' execution had pleased the Jews, Herod Agrippa had Peter arrested, bound in chains and put in prison. However, an angel came to Peter in the middle of the night and miraculously freed him of his chains, and ordered him to go and resume his preaching of the gospel. Herod Agrippa was ablaze with fury and had the prison guards brought before him so he could punish them as painfully as possible for letting Peter escape. But he was prevented from doing so, lest Peter's escape bring harm to anyone. Instead Herod hurried to Caesarea, where he would meet his own downfall. The entire province gathered to greet him, so he put on a resplendent costume woven of gold and silver and entered the theatre early in the day. When the rays of the sun struck the silvery garment, the gleam of the shimmering metal and the reflected brilliance cast a redoubled light upon the spectators. This blinded the eyes of those who gazed upon him, and his artful arrogance deceived them into thinking there was something more than human about him. The voices of the flattering crowd cried, "Until now we thought of you as just a man, but now we avow you are above the nature of man!" Herod Agrippa took pleasure in these eulogies and made no effort to disown the divine honours bestowed upon him. Then, looking up, he spied an angel in the form of an owl, perched on a rope above his head. He had been told by a fortune-teller, when he was in prison before Caligula had him released, that if he ever saw an owl hovering above him, he would have no more than five days to live. He knew this owl was a harbinger of approaching death and addressed the crowds: "Behold, I your god am about to die!" He knew by the fortune-teller's prediction that death would claim him shortly. He was stricken immediately with a pain in his belly and was dead within five days.

Yeshua came to me in a dream and told me I had to leave Lake Mareotis, and leave Egypt immediately. Our lives were in danger, and he would guide my passage to Gaul, my mother's homeland. Although she died when I was just nine years old, she had always spoken to me in her native tongue. There was also a strong Jewish community in Gaul. It was a Roman territory, and therefore pagan, so we would preach the word of our Lord. Yeshua said we would be safe.

I relayed my dream to the apostles and asked them what they wanted to do. Simon the Zealot, James son of Alpheus and Matthias went to Jerusalem, where Simon would become the second bishop of Jerusalem after James, son of Zebedee.   Lake Mareotis was running pretty smoothly; Philo volunteered to be a 'caretaker' - he had eyes and ears in the city which was invaluable to me - I trusted my life with this man.   Our twelve communities throughout Egypt, Cyprus, Turkey, Greece and Sicily were all thriving and the other apostles felt it was time for them to disperse further. And how they travelled! Andrew went to Georgia and Bulgaria, Thomas and Bartholomew went to Syria and on to India, Matthew travelled to Persia and Ethiopia, Peter and Mark advanced as far as Pontus, Galatia, Cappadocia, Betania, Italy and Asia. Philip went to North Africa and Asia Minor, Thaddaeus (Judas son of James) travelled to Edessa and Mesopotamia and Paul went to Croatia, Italy and Spain.

Joseph of Arimathea, my brother Lazarus, my sister Martha and her maid Martilla, my beloved daughter Sarah, now almost ten years old, Mother Mary, Mary Salome, Maximin and Cedonius, who was born blind and had been cured by our Lord, would accompany me to Gaul. Maximin baptized us in the lake before we left.

I will never forget the look on Philo's face as he bade farewell to us. He left Sarah until last and after a long embrace hastened away to hide his tears. Sarah was sorry to say goodbye to him, but she was also excited about our forthcoming voyage to another land - she hadn't left Lake Mareotis since our trip to Rome and she had no recollection of that as she was only a year old! She was like a daughter to him. I promised him I would return one day, with Sarah.

Joseph arranged everything. The provisions, but more importantly, a 46 foot trading boat with a crew of three Egyptians. She became known as 'The Bark of Mary'.

CHAPTER X

August 43 CE: Marseille, Gaul

At dawn on the 9th August 43 CE, we glided silently away from the quay as the crew rowed towards the harbour entrance before raising the sails. There was no farewell party - we did not wish to draw attention to ourselves. Joseph said there was no time to be lost, and was, as always, anxious for mine and Sarah's welfare. No-one could know that Sarah was my daughter - not even the crew. Having been betrayed by John, Joseph said it was prudent to trust no-one for the time being. I said she was my Egyptian handmaiden.

We had packed lightly. I had the original texts in a leather satchel hidden under my cloak. I couldn't let them out of my sight! The three copies would stay in Egypt; one at Lake Mareotis, incarcerated in a wooden crate and buried in a well disguised area of scrub, and the other two at the communities in Nag Hammadi and Oxyrynchus. The apostles had been writing their own accounts, so when the Romans sprang their dawn raid at Lake Mareotis, those would be the ones they would seize.

I also had with me the amphore in which Yeshua changed water into wine at the wedding in Cana. Mother Mary had her mother Anne's ashes with her; she did not want to leave them behind and would find a safe resting place for them when we were settled.

I tried to hide my sadness at leaving - Sarah was overcome with excitement! The sun was slowly appearing over the horizon as we left the harbour and Pharos lighthouse towered above us, making us feel so small and insignificant. The sun was high in the sky before we lost sight of the lighthouse, a safety beacon for all vessels - it must have saved so many lives!

All was well for the first few days. Joseph thought the weather seemed settled, but this could change of course. Joseph was hoping we would be early enough to miss the infamous euroclydon, which we had become well acquainted with on our voyage to Rome. The wind was blowing from the east, at 15-20 knots and filling our sails, so we were sailing with the wind behind us at a steady 6 knots. It was around 1800 miles to our destination, so we would be at sea for 2-3 weeks, all being well.

Then one night the wind got up. It veered and came from the north so we were pounded on the starboard bow by huge waves. There was a lot of shouting from the captain - the fear and panic was palpable. I clutched Sarah to my side and prayed to Yeshua.

The mast broke in two, a deafening sound of splitting wood, crashing down onto the portside oars. Miraculously no one was hurt, but we had no mainsail and had lost three oars. The captain skilfully converted the remains of our mast into a gaff rig. We still had a foresail and there was so much wind our speed had barely dropped. And the captain said we were still sailing in the direction we wanted to go!

Then the rudder broke, so we couldn't steer either. The captain did another makeshift repair, lashing one of the broken oars to the broken rudder.

Sarah started crying - she was frightened, unsurprisingly. She looked imploringly at me with her all-knowing blue eyes and said,

"Are we all going to drown Mother?"

I replied, "We are in our Lord's tender care Sarah. We must keep faith".

Of course it is easy to have faith when everything is going your way, and rather more difficult when you are cold, tired, hungry and frightened. We were tossed around at the mercy of the elements and I lost count of how many nights we didn't see the stars, followed by cloud-filled days when the sun failed to shine. Not on us anyhow...

And then the wind died. We were becalmed; nearly all our food had gone or was perished, soaked in sea water. Doubt always comes from the mind and I found myself considering another scenario; we could starve to death instead of drowning... and our drinking water reserves were minimal. We prayed and we sang hymns which lifted our spirits. There was little else we could do!

Strangely I felt peaceful and calm. I never doubted that Yeshua would ensure we reached Gaul somehow...

Our prayers were answered. A large shoal of mackerel jumped into the boat to fill our hungry bellies, and gentle rain quenched our parched mouths. We were further blessed by a north westerly current which set our listing boat on a course for south Gaul.

The crew said it was a miracle when the captain spotted land! Joseph tied a sack cloth around the top of the gaff rig to attract the attention of any passing fishermen but 'The Bark of Mary', despite her dishevelled appearance, gallantly beached herself, delivering us all safely ashore.

It was late afternoon and the sun was making its way to the horizon. I would be false if I said I wasn't relieved not to spend another night on 'The Bark of Mary'. We gave thanks to our Lord and made our way ashore. The local people seemed bemused by our arrival and incredulous when we told them where we had come from! Joseph asked where we had landed and we were told this was Marseille. Around 600 BCE, Greeks from Asia Minor, now Turkey, left Phocaea to found a city on the Lacydon inlet. The Phocaeans were the first Greeks to make long distance sea voyages; they discovered the Adriatic Sea, Tyrrhenia, Iberia and Tartessos. The Greeks encountered Gallic tribes; Segobriges, Ligurians and Celts, who lived on elevated sites or oppida.

The city was placed under the protection of Artemis, Apollo and Athena whose temples were up in the hills. The Phocaeans exploited Marseille's favourable geographical position, sheltered from the prevailing winds, protected by the Frioul Islands, and close to the Rhone for doing trade with the Gauls. A legend describes the meeting between a Greek sailor, Protis and a Gallic princess, Gyptis. Her father Nannos, king of the Segobriges, gave them Marseille as a wedding gift; the oldest city in France.

The Greeks brought with them their religion, their language, their building techniques, the cultivation of vines and olive trees and commercial products such as wine and Mediterranean ceramic vases. This union gave rise to a rich culture.

In 49 BCE, Julius Caesar conquered the city of Marseille. When the order was issued to them, the people of the city gave up their weapons, took their vessels out of the port and the shipyards, and handed over the money from the treasury. Caesar allowed the city to remain as it was and it retained its Greek character for some time. In the port area there was a paved forum, a traditional Greek theatre and further east a large building housing thermal baths. Large warehouses were built on the northern shore to keep large storage jars for holding grain or wine.

This is where my mother Eucharia had grown up! As promised, Yeshua had brought us all here safely, without a hair harmed on any of our heads!

We took refuge under the portico of a nearby local shrine, whilst the captain and Joseph went to find some food and water for us. We were all exhausted and slept under the wings of God's angels that night, warm and dry.

In the morning, Joseph went with the captain to arrange the crew's passage back to Alexandria - as luck would have it there was a ship leaving later that day and we bade them farewell together with a safe passage!

Meanwhile, the local people started to arrive at the shrine to offer sacrifice to the idols. I stepped forward and, with a few well-chosen words, calmly but fervently preached the word of our Lord to them.

The governor of that province, namely Gaul, Gnaeus Julius Agricola, came with his wife Domitia to offer sacrifice and pray to the gods for offspring, as they had been trying to have a child for some years. I preached Christ to him and dissuaded him from sacrificing. A few days later, I appeared to his wife in a vision, saying,

"Why, when you are so rich, do you allow the saints of God to die of hunger and cold?". I also implored her to persuade her husband to relieve our needs, or she might incur the wrath of God. She was too afraid to tell her husband about the vision. The following night I appeared in the same vision to Domitia and still she hesitated and said nothing to Julius. So the following night I appeared to each of them, shaking with anger, my face afire as if the whole house was burning and said,

"So you sleep, tyrant, limb of your father Satan, with your viper of a wife who refused to tell you what I had said? You take your rest, you enemy of the cross of Christ, your gluttony sated with a bellyful of all sorts of food while you let the saints of God perish from hunger and thirst? You lie here, wrapped in silken sheets, after seeing those others homeless and desolate, passing them by? Wicked man, you will not escape! You will not go unpunished for your long delay in giving them some help!"

And then I disappeared. Domitia awoke, gasping and trembling, and turned to Julius who was in similar distress.

"My lord, have you had the dream I just had?"

"I saw it," he answered, "and I can't stop wondering and shaking with fear! What are we to do?"

"It will be better for us to give in to her than face the wrath of her God she preaches."

And so from that day they invited us to lodge with them. Sarah's eyes were out on stalks as we approached the governor's house - she thought it was a palace! Gleaming in white marble perched on top of a hill overlooking the port; even compared to the majestic buildings I had seen in Alexandria, it was impressive. The entrance was protected by a gold leaf gilded gate, guarded at all times by two Roman legionnaires. The house was set back some distance, with an immaculate driveway flanked by manicured gardens and marble statues. In front of the house was a colonnaded veranda affording shade for meals and siestas. There were at least eight bedrooms, not including the servants' quarters, and Sarah skipped around the house saying she was an Egyptian princess - how right she was! I was grateful, but for me this was just temporary - I had grown up with wealth and it no longer interested me; but served as an interim solution which I was grateful for.

One day when I was preaching, the governor approached and asked me,

"Do you think you can prove the faith you preach?"

"I am ready indeed to prove it," I replied, "because my faith is strengthened by the daily miracles of Peter, who presides in Rome!"

Julius and Domitia then said to me, "We are prepared to do whatever you tell us if you can obtain a son for us from the God you preach about."

"In this he will not fail you" I replied. I prayed to our Lord to grant them a son. My prayers were heard and Domitia conceived.

Julius wished to go to Peter and find out if I was preaching the truth about Christ. Domitia was horrified.

"What's this?" she snapped. "Are you thinking of going without me? Not a bit of it. You leave, I leave. You come back, I come back. You stay here, I stay here!"

The governor replied, "My dear, it can't be that way! You are pregnant and the perils of the sea are infinite. It's too risky. You should stay home and take care of what we have here!"

But she insisted at great length. She threw herself at his feet, sobbing, and in the end won him over. I put the sign of the cross on their shoulders for protection; they stocked a ship with all the necessaries, and left me in charge of their household and their possessions. A day and a night had not passed when the wind rose and the sea became tumultuous. All aboard, especially Domitia, were shaken and fearful as the waves battered the ship. Domitia went into early labour, and exhausted by her pangs and buffeting of the ship, lost consciousness as her son was born. The new born cried continuously, seeking the comfort of his mother's breasts. Julius was overcome with grief and said to himself,

"Alas, what shall I do? I yearned for a son and now I have lost both him and his mother!" Meanwhile the crew were shouting,

"Throw that corpse overboard before we all perish! As long as it is with us, this storm will not let up!"

They seized the body and were about to cast it into the sea, but Julius intervened,

"Hold on!" he cried, "even if you don't want to spare the mother, at least pity the poor weeping little one! Maybe my wife has only fainted and may begin to breathe again!"

Julius spied a hilly coast not far off the bow, and he thought it would be better to put his wife's body and the infant ashore there rather than throw them as food to the sea creatures. His pleas and bribes barely persuaded the captain to drop anchor there. When he went ashore with his wife and son, he found the ground so hard he could not dig a grave, so he spread his cloak in a fold of the hill, laid his wife's body on it, and placed his son's head between his mother's breasts. He named his son Julius and then he wept and said,

"Oh Mary Magdalene, you brought ruin upon me when you landed at Marseille! On your advice I set out on this journey! Did you not pray to God that my wife might conceive? Conceive she did, and suffered death giving birth, and the child she conceived was born only to die as he has no mother to nurse him. Behold, this is what your prayer obtained for me. I commended my all to you and do commend me to your God. If it be in your power, be mindful of my wife's soul, and by your prayer take pity on the child and spare its life."

Then he enfolded the body and the child in his cloak and returned to the ship.

When Julius arrived in Rome, Peter came to meet him, and seeing the sign of the cross on his shoulder, asked him who he was and where he had come from. He told Peter all that had happened to him and Peter responded,

"Peace be with you! You have done well to trust the good advice you received. Do not fret - your wife sleeps and your son rests with her. It is in the Lord's power to give gifts to whom he will, to take away what was given, to restore what was taken away, and to turn your grief into joy."

Peter then took him to Jerusalem and showed him all the places where Christ had preached and performed miracles, as well as where he had suffered and where he had ascended to heaven. Peter then gave him a complete instruction of the faith, and after two years had passed, wished to return to his homeland. He boarded a ship bound for Marseille. By divine will he came close to the hilly coast where he had left his wife and son, and with pleas and money, he persuaded the crew to take him ashore. The little boy, who had been preserved unharmed, used to come down to the beach to play with stones and pebbles, as children love to do. As Julius' skiff drew close to the shore, he saw a boy playing on the beach. He was dumbstruck at seeing his son Julius alive and leapt ashore with great delight. The boy, who had never seen a man, was terrified and ran to his mother's bosom, taking cover under her cloak. Julius approached them slowly, and saw the handsome child feeding at his mother's breast. He lifted the boy and said,

"Oh Mary Magdalene, how happy I would be if my wife were alive and able to return home with me! Indeed I know and believe beyond any doubt, that having given us this child and kept him alive for two years on this rock, you could now, by your prayers, restore his mother to life and health." And as these words were spoken, his wife breathed, and as if waking from sleep, said,

"Great is your merit, oh blessed and glorious Mary Magdalene! As I struggled to give birth, you did me a midwife's service and waited upon my every need like a faithful handmaid."

Hearing this, Julius said, "My dear wife, are you alive?"

"I certainly am," she answered, "and am just coming from the pilgrimage you yourself are returning. And as blessed Peter conducted you to Jerusalem and showed you all the places where Christ suffered, died and was buried, and many other places, I, with blessed Mary Magdalene as my guide and companion, was with you every step of the way!"

Whereupon she recited all the places where Christ had suffered and fully explained the miracles and all she had seen, remembering every detail.

Julius and his family joyfully re-joined the ship and in a short time entered the port of Marseille. Going into the city they found me with my disciples, preaching. Weeping with joy, they threw themselves at my feet and related all that had happened to them, then received holy baptism from Maximin. Their faith was rewarded and shortly after Domitia fell pregnant and in the following year gave birth to a daughter, Julia.

They destroyed the temples of all the idols in the city of Marseille and built churches to Christ. They also elected Lazarus as bishop of the city. Later by the will of our Lord we went to the city of Aix, and by many miracles, led the people there to accept the Christian faith. Maximin was ordained bishop of Aix.

CHAPTER XI

September 45 CE: Avalon

It was Joseph's idea to return to Avalon, which he had discovered some years earlier quite by accident. He said it was an unforgettable place, mystical, and thought it would be the most perfect site to build the first church in England.

After returning from our pilgrimage to Rome, Joseph had sailed to Marseille in 35 CE and then onto Avalon. His plan was to catch up with old business acquaintances in the lead and tin mines - at that time, Britain led the world with its tin mining. He had sailed northward to the northwest coast of Gaul (Brittany,) where through Joseph's contacts, was able to exchange his ocean-going freighting boat for a flatboat to cross the channel and enter the Severn Estuary. Stopping briefly at Guernsey, they proceeded around the coastline of Land's End and the Cornwall coastline. The flatboat was able to negotiate the shallow waters of the Severn Estuary, where they went as far upstream as possible and ran aground on the marshes. They went ashore and found they were at a place called Ynes Witrin, the Celtic name for the Isles of Glass. It was also known as the Isle of Avalon, as it is completely surrounded by marshlands. Isle of Avalon means Island of Fruit Trees.

Joseph and his companions preached the gospel and were treated with cordiality by King Arvivagus of Siluria. The King was greatly taken with Joseph and granted him twelve hides of Glastonbury land - about 1,440 acres.

Joseph wanted to show this special place to me. We set sail from Marseille in the first week of September, accompanied by Mother Mary, Mary Salome, Martha, Martilla and Sarah of course! Sarah would be twelve on the 14th September - so hard to believe! She was a young woman now, mature for her years, beautiful, intelligent and kind. Everything a mother could wish for. She spent a lot of time with Domitia as I was preaching every day. When she was little she could come with me but now she was older it was important she kept up with her education. Domitia had arranged a tutor for her so she was now fluent in French, in addition to the other subjects Philo had started her on in Alexandria.

We followed the same route as Joseph of Arimathea had taken ten years ago and exchanged boats in North West Gaul and crossed the Channel stopping en route in Guernsey. We sailed up the Severn Estuary and went ashore in the Avalon marshes. We climbed a hill to survey the local countryside.

It was known to the locals as the Tor, a Celtic term meaning *A Thin Place*, where the barrier between the earth and spirit world is narrow. Spiritual reality impinges into material reality at these special places, giving one a sense of the connection of spiritual nature with the core of reality, generating a wonderful feeling of peace, wonder and awe.

According to the Celts, Avalon was one of the three *Perpetual Choirs*, the other two were at Stonehenge and Llantwit Major in South Wales. These choirs were referred to as the triad, and in each of these choirs there were 2,400 saints; a hundred for every hour of the day and the night in rotation, perpetuating the praise and service of God without rest or intermission. The purpose of these choirs was to maintain the enchantment and peace of Britain.

The vast watery flatlands and marshy lakes extended to the west as far as the eye could see, reflecting the sky and sun like glass. Maybe this was why the local Celts called this place the *Isles of Glass*.

Joseph had brought with him a staff made from the 'Holy Crown of Thorns' worn by Yeshua. Joseph had in mind another place - a nearby hill not as high as the Tor. I remarked that we were all rather weary and perhaps we should take some refreshment. Joseph exclaimed, "No, this is the place - wait a moment!" He proceeded to thrust the staff into the ground. The thorn staff immediately took root and we named the place 'Wearyall Hill'.

The locals took us in whilst Joseph hired locals to help him build a shelter for us at the bottom of the Tor, amongst the apple trees. There was a spring nearby, so we did not have to carry fresh water far. It was a large round hut made of stone, wood and thatch. The outer wall was made up of a ring of stones supporting a thatched roof. Large, smooth, oak timbers were sunk into the ground encircling a central hearth - after the balmy climate of southern Gaul, we found the English climate cool and damp - we had a fire burning constantly to keep us warm!

Smaller timbers radiated out from a central point at the top to the outer ring of stones at the bottom. All this held the thick reed thatching. Its appearance reminded me of a witch's hat!

Anyway, we were not planning to be there long term - its purpose was to keep us warm and dry which it did admirably. On days when the sun shone, Mother Mary, Mother Salome and I would enjoy a few minutes sitting on a bench under the apple trees admiring the views - the hillside vale, the Tor and Chalice Hill.

Joseph and his hired hands went on to build a church of mud and wattle on a nearby site - a scaled down version of the ancient Tabernacle of Moses. He decreed that twelve monks should always reside in that most sacred place. Joseph dedicated the church to Mary and it was the first church in Britain. In the future there would be some debate as to which Mary this church was dedicated to: Mary Mother of Jesus or myself - in fact it was in memory of all three of us!

Joseph had also brought with him a cup which Yeshua had drunk from at the last supper. Joseph said we had to keep this safe as many treasure hunters would like to get hold of it, so he hid it at the bottom of a nearby well. This became known as the 'Chalice Well', or others call it the 'Blood Well'. Joseph estimated that some twenty thousand gallons of red tinted water pass through the well each day. The red tint is caused by high iron content in the water. It would have healing properties for those who drank from it.

When the church was built Yeshua came to me in a dream and said it was time to return to Gaul and continue our preaching there. Although I would have travelled to India if Yeshua had bid it, I was happy about this - it was my mother's home land and Gaul would become my home for the rest of my time on earth.

CHAPTER XII

December 45 CE: The three Marys disperse

I felt joyful and relieved as we sailed once more into the port of Marseille. We made our way to the residence of Julius and Domitia who were overjoyed to see us again. They lived in luxury and provided for us in every way possible, but I felt my travels were over for the time being and I craved a place of solitude, where I could devote myself to divine contemplation and silently commune with our Lord without interruption. Churches were built in the region presided over by Lazarus as bishop of of Marseille. A nunnery was established and when we left Marseille I gave them the amphore which Yeshua had changed water into wine at the wedding in Cana. They were overjoyed to have something that had been not only handled by Yeshua, but was a famous relic.

La Baume cave

Yeshua led me to a remote cave in La Baume forest, made ready for me by the hands of angels. It was 30 miles or so from Marseille, and a similar distance from Aix where my dear friend Maximin was. The cave was located at the top of a ridge, after a half hour walk uphill through the forest.

Fresh drinking water dripped through the cave ceiling, and our Lord provided my sustenance - the good things of heaven. Every day at the seven canonical hours I was carried aloft by angels and heard with my own ears the glorious chants of the celestial hosts. Day by day I was gratified with these supernal delights and, being conveyed back to my cave by the same angels, needed no material nourishment.

I also went to many places on the etheric places; I would bilocate* to meet Mother Earth's peoples who were much more receptive to Yeshua's teachings than the Jewish people! Yeshua said it was important to continue our energetic work with the consciousness grids of the planet, to plant seeds that one day would germinate.

To trust and know that there would come a day when more hearts were

---

* Quantum mechanics has confirmed that matter can indeed be in two places at once. Through quantum entanglement, particles millions of light years apart can be connected without physical contact.

ready to awaken. To help others to know inner peace, and be as a child who is willing to be innocent, simple and free.

This is what fed *my* soul, but it was clear to us all that it was not a suitable home for my teenage daughter who was still in education. The two Marys would bring her regularly to visit me, but they wanted a place of their own too.

Saintes Maries-de-la-Mer

Joseph of Arimathea took Mother Mary, Mary Salome, Sarah, Martha and Martilla by boat to a small fishing village some 30 miles to the west of Marseille. It was located on the Rhone river delta, about 1km east of the mouth of the Petit Rhone distributary. It was called Ra in the Camargue region, but also known as Notre-Dame-de Ratis (Our Lady of the Boat - 'Ra' being used in 'ratis', or 'boat'). It was later renamed Saintes Maries-de-la-Mer, St Marys-by-the-sea.

The boat beached on a bleak marshy shore at the foot of an oppidum on which there was a Celtic altar, dating back to the 4th century BCE.

The oppidum was a sacred site of the Celtic threefold water goddess and the water source on the island was a holy spring that became known as Oppidum Priscum Ra, named after the Egyptian god Ra, father of the sun. This was the Greek influence, who populated the Camargue as well as Marseille; Marseille had been a Greek city prior to the Roman invasion in 30 BCE, and to all intents and purposes, remained so.

The two Marys and Martha evangelized the region and were greatly received by the local people, who not only provided food and shelter, but also saddled horses whenever they wished to visit me in La Baume cave. The locals made available a small two bedroom house for them to live in; the two Marys shared one bedroom, as they never tired of one another's company and Martha and Sarah shared the other bedroom. Martilla, Martha's maid, slept downstairs in the living room.

As the two Marys were now settled, Mother Mary felt it was time to lay her mother Anne's ashes to rest. She entrusted them to a faithful follower named Auspicius. He placed them in a subterranean grotto in Apt, Provence, some 90 miles from Saintes Maries-de-la-Mer, to protect them from the barbarians. Their location remained secret until their miraculous discovery many years later by a deaf handicapped boy.

Martha and the dragon

Around 48 CE, in the forest along the Rhone between Arles and Avignon, local folklore said there lived a dragon that was half animal and half fish, larger than an ox, longer than a horse, with teeth as sharp as horns and a pair of bucklers on either side of his body. The beast lurked in the river and terrified the local people, killing all those who tried to sail by sinking their vessels and devouring their occupants. The dragon had come from Galatia in Asia, born from a Leviathan, an extremely ferocious water-serpent, and an Onachus, an animal found in the region of Galatia, known to aim its acrimonious dung at pursuers. The local people had heard of the miracles performed by the two Marys and Martha, and implored them for help. Martha volunteered to go, and Martilla accompanied her as they were seldom apart.

They journeyed by boat up the River Rhone, and Martha found the dragon in the forest devouring a man. She slowly approached the animal holding up her cross and sprinkled him with holy water from her pouch. The dragon was immediately subdued and stood still as a statue while Martha used her belt as a halter and placed it over its head. She led him to the people who killed him there and then with lances and stones. The locals called this dragon Tarasconus and, in memory of this event, the place then became known as Tarascon. Prior to this it was known as Nerluc, meaning 'black place', because the local forest was dark and feared by the locals.

After seeking permission from myself and Maximin, Martha and Martilla stayed in Tarascon for the rest of their days, devoting themselves to prayer and fasting. A community of sisters grew around them; they avoided meat, fats, eggs, cheese and wine, took food only once a day, and knelt in prayer over a hundred times a day and night.

One day when Martha was preaching between the town of Avignon and the river Rhone, a youth was standing on the other side of the river and wanted to hear what she was saying. He had no boat, so he undressed and started to swim across. But he underestimated the swift current and was carried away and drowned. It took two days to find his body, which his family brought to Martha and laid at her feet, asking her to bring him back to life. Martha proceeded to lie on the ground, her arms extended in the form of a cross, and prayed,

"Adonai, Lord Jesus Christ, you once raised my brother Lazarus, your friend, to life! , Look upon the faith of these people gathered here, and give life to this boy!"

She took the lad's hand, and to the amazement and delight of the local people, he stood up, and received holy baptism shortly thereafter.

Martha had erected in the nunnery garden a statue of Yeshua wearing a garment similar to the one he had been wearing when she first met him in Bethany, when he cured her of a blood flux. She prayed before it devoutly every day. The grass that touched the hem of the garment was so filled with power that it cured many of their illnesses.

Martilla recorded all these events and asked to be buried alongside her beloved mistress so they would be together in death as they were in life.

One night Yeshua came to me and said he wanted me to return to Alexandria to resume my writing. He also said I should take Sarah with me - he wanted to prepare her for her future and I should fulfil my promise to reunite her with Philo. Philo was approaching seventy, so time was of the essence.

Yeshua also wanted me to visit John in Ephesus, to make peace and reconcile our differences. We were preaching the Way of the Heart after all. For me this was not a problem, but I would need divine intervention to open John's heart.

This came in the form of Mother Mary and Mary Salome. Although they were now 69 and 67 years old respectively, Mother Mary sent word that she and Mary Salome would accompany us to Ephesus. Mother Mary felt she could serve as a useful intermediary - John was more likely to listen to her because he believed Yeshua wanted John to take care of Mother Mary after his death. In fact, Yeshua had entrusted his mother to Joseph of Arimathea as the apostles had gone into hiding after Yeshua's arrest.

Joseph came to La Baume cave on horseback to escort me to Marseille, to the house of the Governor and his family. The governor had sent a boat to Saintes Maries-de-la-Mer to collect the two Marys and Sarah. It was

Sarah's 21st birthday and Domitia had kindly arranged a special dinner for us with her family. Julius was now a healthy ten year old and his younger sister, Julia, eight years old. The children adored Sarah and were going to miss her greatly. She always had time to play with them - games she had been taught by Philo at Lake Mareotis when she was a similar age.

Sarah had brought her boyfriend, Jean Claude du Bois, with her as they would not see one another for some time. I was always excited to see my daughter and she seemed particularly happy on this occasion. I thought it was because of our forthcoming trip to Alexandria, but it was quickly apparent from her eyes which were even brighter than normal, and her demeanour, that there was something else on her mind. She was in love. I had met Jean Claude a few times and liked him very much. He was a cabinet maker and she had met him in the local market where he was working - she was 18 and he was 20. Sarah had a good head on her shoulders and was not looking for a romantic liaison. But she was also stunningly beautiful and Jean Claude had pursued her with great zeal, wile and enthusiasm. He took her horseback riding, fishing and on country walks with a simple picnic he had prepared of local bread, cheese and wine. He wooed her slowly but surely; they were friends for months before it developed into a romance. When Sarah first described him to me she said he had kind, dark brown eyes. He was tall, with shoulder length jet black hair and a close trimmed beard; not to mention handsome, strong, intelligent and he made her laugh. All symptoms I recognized as being in love! Oh it took me back to the day when I met Yeshua in Bethany and my breath was taken away - I had been mesmerised by his unforgettable blue eyes! My older brother Lazarus was a little surprised, but knew better than to try to dissuade me from leaving our home immediately to follow him!

Sarah later told me she was sure he was the one for her when she realized his initials were the same as her father's, J.C. He was also in the same profession as her paternal grandfather, Joseph, who was a carpenter.

Poor Joseph. He never came to terms with the death of his son. He was a broken man. Mother Mary tried in vain to persuade him to come to Egypt with us but he insisted on staying in Jerusalem and became a recluse. I asked Stephen to keep an eye on him - he said he never went out, barely ate or spoke, and if he did it was always about Yeshua and the injustice of his death. Joseph died in his sleep less than a year after Yeshua's crucifixion. Mother Mary believes he died of a broken heart. I could not imagine the immeasurable pain of losing a child, it must be so much worse than any physical pain but something Mother Mary knew only too well.

Jean Claude was ambitious too. He had progressed from selling pieces he had made on a stall at the local market, to having his own shop with a workshop at the rear. He was known for his good quality workmanship, and being both reliable and true to his word, meant his order book was full for at least six months.

I liked the way he looked so nervous when he arrived. He took me to one side and asked if I would give my permission for him to marry my beautiful daughter. She was quite simply the most amazing woman he had ever met! I could not disagree with him on that!

He said he would convert to Judaism; learn Hebrew, pray, observe the Jewish festivals, keep kosher and take Holy bread every Shabbat (Sabbath). A Jewish marriage is traditionally expected to fulfil the commandment to have children (Genesis 1:28) and he said of course their children would be brought up Jewish.

Given her bloodline, I asked him if he was prepared to follow his wife, rather than she follow him. He looked at me very seriously and said he would follow her anywhere in the world as long as he could be with her. If necessary he would sell his business and move anywhere.

I was hopeful that she would take on my work in the not too distant future - Sarah would continue my legacy and he would have to be prepared to support her. I embraced Jean Claude and said assuming Sarah agreed to marry him they could set a date for their wedding on our return from Alexandria. Clearly they had already had that conversation and Jean Claude announced their betrothal (*erusin*) before dinner!

In Jewish law, marriage comprises two separate acts, the betrothal ceremony, and *nissu'in*, the actual Jewish wedding ceremony. These two ceremonies take place up to a year apart; the bride normally lives with her parents until the wedding ceremony , which would take place in a room or tent that the groom had set up for her. After the betrothal, the laws of adultery applied, and the marriage could not be annulled without divorce.

According to the Talmud, the betrothal involves the groom handing an object to the bride, such as a ring, or a document stating that she is betrothed, in the presence of two unrelated male witnesses. Bending tradition to acknowledge the role Mother Mary and Mary Salome had played in Sarah's life, it was only fitting that Sarah asked them to be witnesses, even though they were women. Jean Claude gave Sarah a silver cross necklace to keep her safe and remind her of him whilst she was away in Egypt. She still had the wooden cross Peter had made before we left Egypt in 43 CE - she said it was one of her most precious belongings.

We had the most wonderful happy evening together with delicious food, wine and lots of laughter. I promised to return to our good friends in Gaul with Godspeed. Sarah would not wish to be away a moment longer than she had to be..

CHAPTER XIII

September 55 CE: Ephesus, Turkey

Julius arranged a boat with provisions and insisted on accompanying us with a few of his most trusted men to guard our safety. In consideration of Joseph and particularly the two Marys' advancing years, he wanted them to travel in comfort and the boat he commissioned was luxurious compared to dear little 'Bark of Mary'. His thriving son was a constant reminder of how our Lord had helped his wife to conceive him and then save her life also. For him, two miracles were more than any man's share in a single lifetime and he often said he would be forever in our debt - we were his family. Our needs were modest, but completely met without question. His wife, Domitia, was very close to Sarah, loving her as her own, ensuring she received a good education in the days when girls were raised to make good wives and mothers. Of course it was now apparent she would have that as well, but my wish was that she would have options and make her own choices, not someone else's.

And so Joseph, Mother Mary, Mary Salome, Sarah and I set sail on our voyage to Alexandria via Ephesus. Joseph felt this would be his last voyage. He had sailed to so many countries - he was seventy years old and planning to retire to Compostela in Spain, where dear James was buried. He wanted to spend whatever time he had left in contemplation and prayer and Compostela called to him.

John did not return to Asia after his visit to Jerusalem in July 43 CE after paying respects to his brother James' body. He felt called to go to Rome and became pastor of a church there. The Roman emperor, Claudius, was tolerant of John, given that he had revealed my whereabouts to him. News had reached Claudius that I was now in Gaul, France, evangelizing the local people, including the Governor of Gaul and his wife - but at least I was no longer in his jurisdiction. The Christians were growing worryingly in numbers, but I felt he did not want my blood on his hands.

Pontius Pilate had reluctantly had Yeshua executed and paid a heavy price. After being exiled to Gaul he tragically ended his own life. Whether it was the loss of power and position, guilt, or pressure from his wife who had pleaded with him to spare Yeshua's life, we would never know. Another unnecessary loss of life. Whichever way, it was a lose, lose, situation and the torment was too much for him.

John moved to Ephesus in 48 CE and became pastor of a church there. He also had a special relationship with other churches in the area, he wrote letters to the seven churches in Asia, recorded later in Revelations, whilst in exile in Patmos.

Ephesus (Ephesos, "desirable") was a city of the Roman province of Asia, near the mouth of the Cayster river, three miles from the western coast of Asia Minor, and opposite the Island of Samos. It had an artificial harbour accessible to the largest ships, and rivalled the harbour at Miletus, an ancient Greek city on the western coast of Anatolia. Ephesus stood upon the sloping sides and at the base of two hills, Prion and Coressus, commanding a beautiful view; its climate was exceptionally fine, and the soil of the valley was unusually fertile.

The city was located at the entrance of a valley which reached far into the interior of Asia Minor, and was connected by highways with the chief cities of the province, making Ephesus the most easily accessible city in Asia, both by land and sea. Its location therefore favoured its religious, political and commercial development, and indeed our missionary endeavours.

John always believed Mother Mary would go to live with him and so he built a house for her near Ephesus. But this never happened. Mother Mary and Mary Salome came with me to Gaul. This was another thorn in his side towards me. The 'House of the Virgin Mary' is a stone house located on Mt. Koressos, in the countryside outside Ephesus. Built with rectangular stones, the windows were high up near the flat roof and it consisted of two parts, with a hearth at the centre of the house.

Julius may have been able to choose our ship, but the weather was beyond his control. Thankfully, the winds were fair and blowing from the west which made our passage swift and smooth. We sailed into Ephesus harbour on a bright, sunny Sunday morning. It didn't take long to find John. Joseph asked where the church was - and there he was, preaching to his followers.

John was expecting us. Twenty one years was a long time to arrive unannounced, especially a visitor who he had showed open disloyalty to. I also wrote to John saying Mother Mary wanted to visit him. I think this is why Julius insisted on accompanying us - after having had to flee Egypt and being all but shipwrecked he wasn't taking any chances - John would have to earn his trust. I also mentioned it would give us an opportunity to unify our faith and ensure our teachings were in a similar vein. I truly believed this is what Yeshua would have wanted.

John was overjoyed to see Mother Mary and treated the rest of us with indifference bordering on contempt. He had been called 'son of thunder' for a reason. He was dismissive of Sarah, in his mind a child of a sinner. He confided to Mother Mary that he wasn't even convinced Sarah was Yeshua's daughter! It was as well he did not relay that to me - I would not have been as calm as dear Mother Mary was. Fortunately Sarah didn't get to hear these hurtful untruths.

He refused to discuss anything with me. Mother Mary had been right about coming along - she was the only one he would talk to. Despite his high office, Julius failed to impress John as he was loyal to me. Oh how I hated these divisions, but I felt powerless! All he wanted to do was show Mother Mary the house he had built for her - he said he had been waiting for her and had never given up hope. He begged Mother Mary to stay with him so he could fulfil his promise to Yeshua. Mother Mary felt compassion for him and when she agreed to stay with him whilst Joseph, Sarah and I were in Egypt, he softened a little. They both had hopes; he that Mother Mary would fall in love with the place and spend the rest of her days there, Mary hoped to convince John of my worthiness and heal the rift between them. I was doubtful. Mother Mary was adamant that Mary Salome would stay with her too, as they were all but inseparable. This was not entirely to John's pleasure, but he could see this had already been decided, so he didn't argue. After all, he had what he had wished for - Mother Mary.

I felt I had failed in my mission and prayed to Yeshua that night for guidance. He came to me in a dream and said I had done all I could do for now - the Way of the Heart called for love, patience and forgiveness. I thought of Yeshua's words as he was dying on the cross; "Forgive them for they know not what they do", and I felt humbled. My setbacks were mere irritations compared to my beloved's suffering.

There was no reason for us to stay - our presence was not required or desired and so as soon as our ship was restocked, John bade us farewell and we resumed our journey to Alexandria. I told the two Marys I would return as soon as I could but that it would be months not weeks - I wasn't sure what or how much Yeshua had in mind for me to write at that point.

CHAPTER XIV

October 55 CE: Lake Mareotis

Philo was the first to emerge from the communal building when we arrived back at Lake Mareotis. He stopped in his tracks and for a moment he was speechless, which was rare for our eloquent Philo. His expression was a sight to behold and he all but sank to his knees when Sarah ran to embrace him. They hugged for a long time - Philo kept on taking her by her shoulders to look her in the face, with tears of joy rolling down his cheeks, and then embracing her as if he wasn't going to let her out of his sight again. He knew this was just a visit, and he was going to savour every moment. He had waited twelve years for this moment! It goes without saying that Philo had missed Sarah more than she had missed him. He repeatedly said how beautiful she was! Sarah touched hearts wherever she went - Yeshua would truly be proud of the beautiful, kind, accomplished, woman she had become. And so was I!

Sarah told Philo that she was betrothed to a wonderful man from Gaul called Jean Claude and that he must come to the wedding. The look in his eyes gave his answer - he had been suffering from a weak heart and his doctors would discourage him from travelling that far (although in my estimation he was 66 and younger than the two Marys!). Sarah wasn't taking no for an answer,

"Who is going to tutor our children then?"

"So you haven't changed much," Philo replied, shaking his head, "dead set on getting your own way - you have been like that since you were three years old!"

Then they both collapsed into gales of laughter, just like the old times.

James (son of Alpheus), Simon the Zealot and Matthias had travelled from Jerusalem to see us; they waited patiently in the background until the excitement of the reunion between Philo and Sarah had subsided.

Our community was in good order, it was now 22 years old, and numbers had swelled to 180!

News of our enforced exile from Egypt had attracted interest and sympathy from local men and women from all walks of life - James, Simon and Matthias had been arrested and imprisoned in Alexandria but the erroneous charges made against them were dropped after public outcry, with demonstrations in the agora and outside the prison from Egyptians, Greeks and Jews alike. It was in the Romans' interest to keep the peace in Alexandria as it was so important economically to fund the Roman Empire. The apostles were released unharmed and there were spontaneous celebrations in the streets of the city. Their incarceration was somewhat counterproductive; our community had a surge of visitors in the following weeks and months!

Peter founded the church in Antioch, Syria in 45 CE, and then went to Rome under Emperor Claudius to oppose Simon Magus. He preached there and became Bishop of Rome. Paul preached the gospel in Illyricum (Croatia), Italy and Spain, before joining Peter in Rome.

It was a sad day when we heard that Peter and Paul had been martyred in Rome on the same day in January 56 CE, under the orders of Nero. Luke and Mark witnessed both executions.

As a Roman, Paul received a superior execution by way of beheading. When Paul reached the place of execution, he looked up to heaven, marked his forehead and breast with the sign of the cross, and said,

"My Lord Jesus Christ, into your hands I commend my spirit!"

He received the martyr's crown as the executioner made his stroke and cut off Paul's head. Luke and Mark took Paul's body, embalmed him with sweet spices and buried him.

When Peter came to his cross, he said, "Because my Lord came down from heaven to earth, his cross was straight up; but he deigns to call me from earth to heaven, and so my cross should have my head towards the earth and my feet pointing towards heaven. I am not worthy to be on the cross the way my Lord was, so turn my cross and crucify me head down!"

At the sight of this the people were enraged, and wanted to kill Nero and free the apostle, but Peter pleaded with them not to hinder his martyrdom.

The Lord opened the eyes of those weeping there, and they saw angels standing with crowns of roses and lilies, and Peter standing with them at the cross, receiving a book from Christ and reading from the book, spoke these words:

"You, Lord, are all things to me. I give you thanks with the whole spirit by which I live, understand, and call upon you!"

Peter, knowing that the faithful had seen his glory, gave thanks, commended the faithful to God, and breathed forth his spirit. Mark and Luke took his body down from the cross and buried it embalmed with sweet spices alongside Paul.

Many people saw Peter and Paul clothed in shining garments and wearing crowns with light on their heads. Because of this many of them believed in the Lord and became Christians.

It was prudent that Mark and Luke should leave Rome for the time being - Mark brought Peter's notes with him. Matthew arrived a few weeks later as he had been preaching in Parthia, which later became known as Iran.

Mark founded the church in Alexandria and became the first Bishop of Alexandria. Philo said that from the time of Mark's arrival he brought a great multitude of pagans to the faith of Christ. Mark encouraged them not only by performing prodigious miracles and his eloquent teaching, but by his illustrious example of living.

Mark was a well-built man of middle age, with a long nose, fine eyes, and a heavy beard, balding and greying at the temples. He was reserved in character and full of grace. He was so humble that he amputated his own thumb so he was no longer eligible to be promoted to the priesthood.

When Mark arrived in Alexandria, his shoe fell apart, and Mark saw a spiritual meaning. He declared, "Truly God has cleared the road for me and has not allowed Satan to put obstacles in my way, since my dead works were already forgiven by our Lord."

Mark saw a cobbler mending some old boots and gave him his shoe to be repaired; but in the course of his work the cobbler gravely wounded his left hand and exclaimed aloud, "One of God!"

Mark heard this and said, "Truly the Lord has prospered my journey!".

He made clay with his spittle and spread it on the cobbler's hand, which was healed in an instant. The cobbler took Mark into his own house and closely questioned him about who he was and where he came from. Mark told him he was a servant of our Lord Jesus. The cobbler said,

"I would like to see him!"

Mark replied, "I will show him to you!"

And he began to instruct him about Christ. The cobbler was baptized along with the whole of his household. This man was named Anianus.

Some men of the city heard that some Galilean had arrived and was denouncing the cult of the gods, and they began to plot against him. Mark knew this, so he ordained Anianus and made him Bishop of Alexandria. Mark came to Lake Mareotis and remained with us for some months until my writing was complete.

And then it was as before, when we first came to Lake Mareotis, the words just flowed from Yeshua and I wrote six days a week, from dawn until sunset. It was a glorious feeling to be in such close contact with him every day. If I didn't understand something I had written, I would meditate on it and receive clarification. I felt so alive! I would discuss my transmissions in great detail and consult with the apostles. Yeshua transmitted four gospels in twelve months; which were assigned to Mark, Matthew, Luke and John. The gospels of Mark, Matthew and Luke were assigned to each apostle and they each made three copies of their own gospel. John was not there of course, so Sarah made three copies of the Gospel of John.

When their assistance was no longer required, the apostles left to preach the gospel once again. Mark went to Pentapolis in Italy and preached there for two years. On his return to Alexandria he built a church on the rocks near the sea, at a place called Bucculi, where he found that the number of the faithful had swelled considerably.

Luke, a Syrian born in Antioch and practitioner in medicine, returned to Asia Minor where he remained for the rest of his days.

Matthew remained in Egypt and one day was preaching a sermon about the glory of the earthly paradise, telling the people it had stood above all the mountains and had been close to heaven. That in it there were no thorns or brambles, lilies and roses did not wither, that old age never came, the angels played upon their instruments, and when the birds were summoned, they came at once. Matthew went on to say that mankind had been expelled from this earthly paradise, but through the birth of Christ they had been recalled to the paradise of heaven.

Suddenly a loud cry of mourning arose from the crowd, mourning the death of the king's son. When the sorcerers could not revive him, the apostle Matthew was called for, who by his prayer restored the youth to life. The king, whose name was Egippus, sent a message through his kingdom saying,

"Come and see God hiding in the likeness of a man!".

People came, bringing gold crowns and offerings to sacrifice to Matthew, but Matthew stopped them, saying,

"What are you doing? I am not a god but a servant of the Lord Jesus Christ!"

He persuaded them to use the gold and silver they had brought to build a great church. They completed the church in thirty days, and Matthew presided there for fourteen years until his death in 70 CE at the age of 72, by which time he had converted much of Egypt.

Yeshua said it was time for me to write a gospel in my own name, so in the future people knew who I really was. My mind protested, but I followed my soul and wrote The Gospel of Mary. Sarah made copies for me. Finally, I wrote the Secret Gospel of Mark, which Sarah also copied for me. Then we bound the papyrus leaves together into leather codices as before and put the copies into the underground safe box we had hurriedly prepared in the grounds before we left for Gaul.

When Sarah was not transcribing she made herself useful and got involved in all aspects of running Lake Mareotis. There was a lot of work to run a community of this size, but there were many pairs of willing hands and we shared the work equally amongst the men and women without disagreement. A simple, easy, fulfilling life.

She also spent a lot of time with Philo - there was such a bond between them. They would often work together, although Philo was not very strong and so was relieved from doing any strenuous work. They spent hours in the kitchen, baking bread or washing up, Sarah telling Philo all about the education she received in Gaul. She loved to engage in healthy philosophical debate with Philo and thrived on the intellectual stimulation he gave her. They loved to be outdoors too of course. They would go for a walk every day, how far depended on how Philo was feeling. Philo had a staff but would 'forget' to take it, so would have to link arms with Sarah! Sarah taught him to fish, either from the lake shore, or sometimes they would take a boat out to one of the islands. They would cook it together over a fire on feast days and share it with those members of the community who felt inclined to eat flesh. Sarah never mentioned it, but I think she found the diet of bread and water a little restrictive after the food in Gaul that she was used to!

Sarah must have missed Jean Claude desperately but she never complained about being separated from him for just over a year. This was Philo's time. They would never have this opportunity again and they both knew it. Philo was not afraid of dying, 'a new beginning' he used to say, laughing!

And then Yeshua came to me one night and said my writing was finished for now. I left the three copies of each gospel with monasteries close to Alexandria where we had loyal friends and followers. I would take the originals with me to Gaul. The world was becoming increasingly uncertain and book burning was not uncommon. Safety in numbers, hopefully...

In September 55 CE we left Alexandria once again and headed to Ephesus to collect the two Marys. I had the texts in my leather satchel under my cloak. We were in the safe hands of Julius, his security men and a fine ship which Joseph was greatly impressed with.

I could not bear to watch Philo say goodbye to Sarah. He said he may have been her tutor, but she had taught him the biggest lesson of all - God's greatest gift, love... She had given him more happiness in the few years they had spent together than all the other years put together.

Sarah was still crying when we passed Pharos lighthouse and then she suddenly sat bolt upright and stopped. She did not look back again. Self-pity was a luxury we had seldom indulged in.

CHAPTER XV

October 56 CE: Marseille, Gaul

A favourable southerly breeze filled our sails and we entered Ephesus harbour five days later - we were here to collect the two Marys on our way home to Gaul. Sarah did not mention Philo on the boat - I recognized something of myself in her. I push uncomfortable memories to the back of my mind, but they invariably surface at night of course, and I could hear muffled whimpering whilst she slept. The mind is clever and finds a way of reminding you, however disciplined you are when you are awake. We never discussed Philo or their times together, she was too raw. Thank goodness she had someone waiting for her in Gaul.

Sarah and I were excited to see them, hear their news and see if John's anger had softened towards me. Not a bit of it...Mother Mary's decision to come back to Gaul with us fuelled it even more. He could not even look at me as Julius' men carried their belongings onto our ship.

Mother Mary embraced John - I think they both knew it would be the last time they saw each other, unless John visited her in Gaul which seemed highly unlikely. She felt sad, we all did. It would have upset Yeshua to see such discord amongst his disciples...we had to stay united - we had enough enemies as it was. John was isolating himself, and he would have his own challenges in the not too distant future. Mother Mary spoke little of her stay in Ephesus - she spent most of her time with Mary Salome praying and meditating in the house John had built. It was a few hours walk from John's church, although they made best efforts to attend Sunday morning service to show their support and respect for John. Mother Mary never said a word against John, but I could see sadness and disappointment in her face as we left Ephesus harbour once again. She too felt she had failed.

The weather was kind and we had a pleasant and uneventful two week voyage to Marseille. The Gaul flag on top of our mast alerted the locals to the return of the Governor's ship and so there was quite a gathering at the port quay as we came alongside. Domitia and the children were the first to greet us, delighted to see us all, but especially happy to see Sarah. They were hoping we would stay with them for at least one night, but the two Marys and Sarah were anxious to return home to Saintes Maries-de-la-Mer.

The children looked crestfallen, so Sarah promised she would see them soon. In fact it would be just a few weeks...

And so Julius' ship left safe harbour once more to make the 30 mile trip west along the coast to Saintes Maries-de-la-Mer, where Jean-Claude eagerly awaited the return of his beloved. Mother Mary later recounted to me that the captain dropped anchor as close as he could and they went ashore by skiff. Someone spotted the Governor's flag and Jean Claude was waiting on the beach when they arrived - it was quite a reunion - Jean Claude and Sarah held each other for a long time and they both wept with joy. The locals clapped enthusiastically - they had a special affection for the two Marys and Sarah. And beautiful Sarah was marrying one of their own, so they felt particularly attached to this little trio from Judea.

Sarah and Jean Claude's wedding

Jean Claude and Sarah were married within two weeks - they couldn't bear to be apart any longer. The guest list was short; Lazarus, Julius, Domitia and the children, Jean-Claude's parents, Martha, Martilla, Maximin and a handful of their close friends made us an intimate party of twenty!

The small wooden church in Saintes Maries-de-la-Mer had had been built a few years earlier. It was known as the Church of Mary after Mother Mary. It was set back a little way on higher ground overlooking the shoreline, in the centre of Saintes Maries-de-la-Mer. It had its own spring inside the church, so living water was available for baptisims. The local people had asked for it and raised the funds to build it; somewhere where they could come and hear teachings, pray, worship, seek community, alms, healing or even shelter.

We were Jewish but Sarah and Jean Claude wanted to get married in our Christian church. So they decided to blend the two; a simple ceremony to complete the formalities in the Church of Mary, followed by a reception and enactment of 'The Song of Songs' at the home of Mother Mary and Mary Salome.

'The Song of Songs' is an ancient love poem from the Jewish scriptures that legend says Queen Sheba gave to King Solomon. At the Temple of Isis School I had been taught to understand it on levels beyond the ordinary mind, requiring a different way of seeing. I had shared this knowledge with

Sarah during our time together in Alexandria. The poem could have been written for them. It prepares the couple for conceiving a child in a space of love and light. As Sarah had been... It involves the anointing of the Bridegroom to prepare him to enter the Bride's sacred chamber where they will open to one another. In union, they bring Heaven's great light into the Earth Mother's body. It is a sacred blessing upon all life, so all beings may be abundantly fertile and happy.

The betrothal time gave the women folk, namely Mother Mary, Mary Salome and Domitia, time to prepare the wedding garments. Sarah's skirt was woven from Egyptian white cotton. It was decorated with little bells, shells, stones and silver pieces tied to it. Her long sleeved blouse barely met the waistband of her skirt, so that when she raised her arms, her tanned slim midriff was exposed. It had long draping sleeves which quivered in the breeze and spread like the wings of an angel when she danced. Domitia offered to lend her some of her fine jewellery, but she insisted on wearing her silver cross necklace and that alone. Her long, wavy, dark hair was tied up in a bun with slides made from shells collected from the beach.

Sarah wore a long scarf on her head made of the same fabric as her skirt, held in place by a simple silver headband. The headband was decorated with garlands of sweet roses and jasmine. She looked like an angel, to me anyway!

Sarah chose not to wear any make-up but her tanned face framed her iridescent blue eyes and she shone with a luminance rarely seen in a mere mortal. Within her eyes there was a gentle quality but also a passionate fire - she was a strong young woman with a good head on her shoulders. Her natural beauty took my breath away; simplicity had been the only way of life she had ever known. Or maybe the stories of my early days when clothes, jewellery and perfume were highly prized by me, made her shy away. I felt at 21 she was old enough to hear the whole story of my past, and we had plenty of time on our travels for heart to heart discussions. Better to hear the truth from me rather than a distorted version from someone who had ill feeling towards me. There would be many, now and in the future. Perhaps it was as well that I did not know at this time how distorted my life history would become, and how long it would take for the truth to be revealed...But when you are no longer of this world, time does not exist, and so human emotions such as impatience and frustration are not in the picture. And you can't hide the truth forever.

Jean Claude's mother made him a loose fitting simple white robe of fine linen which showed off his tanned muscular body. He had tied back his jet black wavy shoulder length hair and shaved off his beard, making him look even more handsome.

As soon as we had returned from Alexandria, Mother Mary and Mary Salome barely had time to rest before setting to work on the wedding feast - they were very excited about it all, clucking around like two mother hens. They asked Sarah to bring back spices from Egypt not readily available and far more expensive in Gaul.

Julius and Domitia had insisted on paying for the wedding, saying Sarah and Jean Claude should spare no expense. But we had been frugal for so many years, and shied away from extravagance. It was still expensive! The tent hire, wedding feast, wedding garments and hire of local musicians, singers and horse drawn chariot all added up - we couldn't have possibly afforded it and we accepted, graciously, I hope!

My brother Lazarus, now Bishop of Marseille, officiated at the church ceremony. It took place on Saturday 31st October at 4pm.

Sarah had asked Julius to give her away - he had been like a father to her and treated her as if she were his own daughter. He almost cried with tears of joy when she asked him.

The two Marys wept and I choked back my tears when Sarah entered the church on the arm of Julius - part of her shawl was draped over her face and yet her beauty still radiated with the intensity of a thousand suns. Jean Claude stood at the front of the church alongside his elder brother, Philippe, who was the best man. As Julius unlinked arms with Sarah so she could stand alongside Jean Claude, he turned and looked at her with complete and utter adoration - I smiled to myself as I recognized the purity of his love. They had found union within themselves by balancing the Divine Masculine and the Divine Feminine and therefore union with God, meaning they could come to a relationship full, and have love and light to offer a partner. This kind of love was rare and could be sustained for a life time. They would be happy, not without challenges, but nothing they could not overcome.

Lazarus read out the marriage vows and then nodded at Jean Claude to lift the shawl from in front of her face. Philippe, the best man stepped forward to give the ring to Jean Claude to place on his bride's finger. I looked across at Mother Mary and Mary Salome - unsurprisingly they were crying again - tears of pride and joy!

Lazarus came to the end of the ceremony and announced they were now man and wife. Jean Claude kissed Sarah tenderly on her rose coloured lips and the assembled congregation clapped heartily!

We followed the bride and the groom out of the church and our mini procession filed along the cobbled streets to the two Marys' house for the reception. They were cheered by the locals - we were well known here, and liked! As we approached the house we were greeted by the sound of musical instruments; cymbals, tambourines, drums, flutes, horns, maracas and stringed instruments. As their house was small, a tent had been erected in the courtyard at the rear of the property. We filed through the house to be greeted at the tent entrance by the radiant bride and groom. When we had all congratulated the couple and embraced one another, Sarah and Jean Claude got up for the first dance. We joined hands and made a circle around them dancing, laughing and singing.

Cushions were laid around low tables decorated with vases of sweet smelling roses, lilies, jasmine and lavender. Julius and Domitia brought their kitchen staff with them to help prepare and serve the food - I felt somewhat uncomfortable with this but it was an offering and they did it with love - they all knew Sarah and Jean Claude well and would have been disappointed if they had not been asked, so I accepted their offering with grace and gratitude.

There was special bread, cheese, dried fig and nut meats, a variety of sweets made from honey and date paste, fresh fruit, goat's milk and new wine.

The ceremony began at dusk. Adjoining the dining area was a smaller tent which was the bridal chamber containing the wedding bed. A crimson velvet curtain was tied back across the entrance so we could see inside. There was a raised platform under a red silk canopy that was tied in such a way as to reveal a bed of richly upholstered cushions covered with deep red velvet.

Sarah led the ceremony - she was going to anoint her king. Sarah removed her shoes and blouse to reveal a close fitting, sleeveless white lace bodice, showing her beautiful slim arms, neckline and the contours of her firm breasts. She led Jean Claude to a long wooden bench at the foot of the bed and he sat down. Sarah kneeled at his feet. She lowered her head and gently kissed his feet, her long hair now untied and cascading over his feet.

Sarah then stood up, removing a sealed alabaster vial of precious spikenard oil from the waistband of her skirt. The heat from her body had made the thick syrupy texture warm and easy to pour. After breaking the wax seal, she poured some of the oil onto Jean Claude's head. There was a deafening silence in the room. She placed her hands on his crown, and massaged his now untied hair sensuously, her eyes closed and gently swaying and undulating. Sarah knelt once again at her beloved's feet and poured some oil on them. The drums and percussion started to sound a slow, soft, rhythm accompanied by a chorus of voices.

A cantor* then recited the 'Song of Songs' as Sarah tenderly lifted each anointed foot into her lap and massaged them slowly and methodically, every toe and in between, the soles, every inch of his feet before moving to his ankles. She then reached to his calves, his inner thighs, applying more oil as she rose up his body. His head went back with his eyes closed, breathing deeply and audibly as his passion was awakened. The energy of the music rose and our voices made the sound of a cooing chorus of doves. A soprano joined the male voice, creating beautiful harmonies.

The voice of the Divine Feminine, the Queen of heaven and earth, called forth the King of kings to make his descent. She called in the winds from their four directions. She called the angels of earth, fire, water and air to bear witness. She anointed his head once more, tenderly massaging his face and upper body.

She took his hands and kissed them long and hard. She placed his hands upon her hips and pulled his head towards her bosom. Placing one hand on his crown and the other at the base of his spine, she started to awaken his kundalini and energy started to move up his spine making him shudder.

---

* A cantor is a person who leads people in singing, or sometimes in prayer. He or she sings solo verses or passages to which the choir or congregation responds

Her brown skin glistened with perspiration as she held him close undulating in time with the music. The energy in the room was palpable.

We were all feeling the serpent energy rise in our spines and our faces were moist with tears. What she was doing to him was echoed in our own bodies. The beloved song of ecstasy awakens passion within our hearts and loins. She, the Great Mother, was anointing and awakening her children.

Jean Claude rose to his feet, his robe clinging to his oiled body, the contours of his form visible through his robe. He took Sarah's hands and guided her to sit on the bench - it was the Bride's turn to be anointed. As he anointed her, we could feel the Great Mother offering up her waters, quenching all beings' thirst. As he anointed her hands, heart and stomach, we felt a fiery energy rising up from Mother Earth's core. It rose towards the heavens, merging with the stars and the planets in the universe.

The music reached a crescendo as the male and female voices intertwined, high and low, in solo and duet, like a dance, coaxing an ever rising flow of energy. Sarah and Jean Claude were now standing gazing into each other's eyes, bathing in love, with their right hand on the other's heart, and their left hand on top of the other's right hand. A tunnel of bright light surrounded them and ascended into the heavens. This was tantric alchemy - they were dedicating their joyful, healing, sexual energy to the awakening and happiness of all of us. We were all One.

Then suddenly a musician struck some cymbals together and the music stopped. There was a united gasp from us all, and time stood still for a moment. Then four of Jean Claude's friends rushed forward to raise the bride and groom on their shoulders! The band started up again and we formed a circle around them once more, all of us in ecstasy, dancing, dancing, spinning in the light, faster and faster, weaving in and out of one another without clashing, like the planets orbiting around the sun. The spinning freed our souls, and we were no longer in our minds, we were united, all as one.

There was so much laughter. More wine was poured. Trays of food appeared - fresh fruit and more sweet delicacies! It was dark outside now and the stars shone brightly, as if the Divine Father was celebrating what was happening here on Mother Earth.

It was time for Sarah and Jean Claude to retire to the bridal chamber for the Sacred Union. Sacred Union involves the uniting and merging of Love, Power and Wisdom through sexuality, the heart and consciousness. It is a form of alchemy, bringing love and light to the world, greater than the two could bring as individuals - Sacred Alchemy.

There was an intoxicating myriad of scents; burning frankincense and sandalwood, fused with the pungent smell of the spikenard oil drifting out of the bridal chamber. We watched Sarah untie the canopy veils and the heavy red silks unfurled. The wedding bed was now hidden from view.

Sarah took Jean Claude by the hand and led him into the bridal chamber, drawing the crimson curtain behind her so they were no longer in view. They would reappear at dawn when their marriage had been consummated in love and light.

The band played and we sang, danced and spun all night, reminiscent of our days at Lake Mareotis. We were so energised sleep was far from our minds, for we were in our souls connecting with the union of the Divine Feminine and Divine Masculine. For the soul never tires, only the mind.

When dawn, came Sarah and Jean Claude emerged from the bridal chamber hand in hand looking beatific. They had changed into simple white robes, and there was an aura of light around them so they looked from another world.. We broke into rapturous applause. They embraced us all and made their way to a horse drawn chariot which was waiting outside. The two Marys shed more than a few tears as they watched them leave, even though they were only going a few hundred yards. Waving until out of sight, they made their way to Jean Claude's home above the furniture workshop, where he would carry her over his threshold. Their married life had begun..

It was a truly wonderful day and night - Yeshua would have been so proud of his daughter..

End of an era: The two Marys go home

Julius escorted me back to La Baume cave the day after the wedding. I was keen to get back to my sanctuary and spend time praying, meditating and continuing my work. I would not be travelling overseas again - those days were over.

Now Sarah was settled, the two Marys felt their work in the name of our Lord was over and so could return to him. Inseparable in life, it was not surprising they both died peacefully within three weeks of one another; I took Mary Salome to the light on 21st December 56 CE and Mother Mary on 12th January 57 CE.

Sarah was surprised I did not attend the funerals. I did not need to, I had seen them greeted by a chorus of angels and the loving arms of Yeshua. Sarah felt I should have been there out of respect for them, as we had been through so much together over the last thirty years. But funerals are for those left behind and tears are for oneself not for the departed - we should be wishing our loved ones well on their journeys! I knew exactly where they were and how happy they were. Still together, just without their bodies.

Of course, in my absence over the years, the two Marys were mother figures to Sarah - she had lived with them for most of our time in Gaul, and she felt the loss greatly. What Sarah was *really* saying was that, once again, I was not there for her - she was not my priority. I had delegated my maternal duties. I could not disagree with her...

I am sure the two Marys had waited until she was happily married - their souls had been longing to go for some time. They were both buried in the church in Saintes Maries-de-la-Mer where Sarah and Jean Claude were recently married.

Joseph of Arimathea was now 73 years old and thinking of retirement. His son Simon had been running his business for some time and his wife had died long ago shortly after we built the community at Lake Mareotis.

He had always kept watch over his younger sister Mary Salome and so after the passing of the two Marys he felt free to retire to a monastery in Compostela, Spain, for the rest of his life. He had stumbled on this place on his tin trading travels and always wanted to return there.

As Yeshua had entrusted me into his care, he came to see me to ask my permission and blessing. This I gave without hesitation. My brother Lazarus was now Bishop of Marseille and Maximin was Bishop of Aix. Not coincidentally, La Baume cave was conveniently located about half way between the two. I was well cared for, both on earth and in heaven.

His son Simon collected him from Marseille old port on 21st March 57 CE for his final voyage to Vigo on the north western coast of Spain, the nearest port to Compostela. Julius and Domitia were there to bid him farewell. I heard later that he settled well and lived there very happily for two years - the monks wrote to us to say what a blessing he had been, and how they felt very privileged Joseph had chosen Compostela for his retirement and as his final resting place. He had died in his sleep with a smile on his face and his hands in prayer position on his chest.

It should not have been a shock when Sarah received a letter from Alexandria to say that beloved Philo had died from a heart attack in October the same year. That was the fourth member of her extended family she had lost in just ten months. She cried for Philo. They had such a connection. What a gift he was...I think she loved and respected him above all others - he was like a grandfather to her. She came to me and sobbed in my lap - something I had never seen her do. I felt powerless and prayed to Yeshua to comfort her. Losing loved ones can be very unsettling as I knew only too well...

Sarah threw herself into helping Jean Claude with his business, running the retail side, taking orders, and doing the accounts. Jean Claude could concentrate on what he did best - working with his hands. They were a formidable team and the business flourished. Sarah preached in the local church and once a month they would visit me. They would sail in Jean Claude's boat to Marseille, where they would overnight with Julius and Domitia. Their hospitality for our extended family knew no bounds, and of course the children were always delighted to see Sarah. Julius became very fond of Jean Claude - although they were from very different backgrounds, they would enjoy animated discussions on business and politics long into the night. Sarah was a princess in Julia's eyes and could do no wrong - Julia said she wanted to be like her when she grew up. The following morning Sarah and Jean Claude would ride to La Baume forest and up to my cave. Sarah always brought me homemade bread, as she said I did not eat enough. I always accepted it graciously but never touched it. I gave it to the birds, who were much more appreciative than I was, singing for hours with sheer joy bursting from their little hearts.

I was delighted when Sarah came to me to tell me she had fallen pregnant and on 11th February 58 CE she gave birth to a daughter, at home in Saintes Maries-de-la-Mer. The continuation of Yeshua's bloodline was assured. They named her Mary, not surprisingly, and they wanted me to come and baptize her at their local church. Julius came to collect me - such a good and considerate man, like a son to me. She was beautiful of course, with her father's dark hair and her mother's bright blue eyes. As I held 'little' Mary, memories of the joy I felt holding my own daughter came flooding back.

Every mother feels that their new born child is a miracle - nature is clever at ensuring survival of the human race! I had not been a perfect mother - obviously I loved my daughter, but I had not always been there for her. She had never criticized me openly, but I suspected her approach to motherhood would be very different.

This would be the last time I would leave my cave at La Baume. Not even to visit my second granddaughter Anne, born on 12th September 59 CE. Sarah told me she looked like me, with auburn hair and hazel brown eyes. I would have liked to have paid my respects to my new granddaughter, for Sarah's sake. My spirit was strong, but my body was not, living in a damp cave had given me rheumatism. Sarah tried to persuade me to come and live with her at the coast, saying the air would be much better for me, but I was happy here and wanted to end my days here.

There was a certain priest who also wanted to live a solitary life and built himself a cabin near La Baume cave. One day Yeshua opened the priest's eyes, and he saw how the angels descended to my cave, lifted me into the air and an hour later brought me back with divine praises. Wanting to learn the truth about this wondrous vision and praying to his Creator, he hurried with daring and devotion to my cave. When he was a stone's throw away, his knees began to wobble, and he was so frightened that he could hardly breathe. When he backed away his legs responded, but every time he turned around and tried to approach my cave, his body went limp and his mind went blank, and he was rooted to the spot.

The priest realized there was a heavenly secret there, to which human experience could have no access. He invoked our Saviour's name and called out,

"In the name of our Lord, if you are a human being living in that cave, answer me and tell me who you are!"

When he had repeated this three times, I answered him,

"Come closer, and you can learn the truth about whatever your soul desires."

Trembling, he had ventured halfway towards my cave when I said to him, "Do you remember what the gospel says about Mary the notorious *sinner*, who washed the Saviour's feet with her tears and dried them with her hair, and earned forgiveness for all her misdeeds?"

"I do remember," the priest replied, "and almost thirty years have gone by since then. Holy Church also believes and confesses what you have said about her."

"I am that woman," I said. "For almost twenty years I have lived here unknown to everyone; and as you were allowed to see yesterday, every day I am borne aloft seven times by angelic hands, and have been found worthy to hear with the ears of my body the joyful jubilation of the heavenly hosts.

Now it has been revealed to me by our Lord that I am soon to depart from this world, so please go to blessed Maximin in Aix and inform him that next year, in 63 CE, on the day of the Lord's resurrection, at the time when he regularly rises for matins, he is to go alone to his church, and there he will find me present and waited upon by angels."

To the priest, my voice sounded like the voice of an angel, but he saw no one. The priest hurried to Aix to find Maximin and carry out his errand. Maximin was overjoyed, and gave fulsome thanks to our Lord and awaited the appointed hour and day.

And so in the following months, as I knew my time left on earth was short, I wrote down, with the divine aid of Yeshua, a record of what happened to me in the thirty years following the crucifixion.

I also enclosed a letter addressed to the head librarian at the Serapeum in Alexandria introducing my daughter Sarah, requesting her admission to the Mystery School of Akhenaten.

These I would personally hand to Sarah for safekeeping - she would know what to do with them.

Mary Magdalene,
La Baume Cave, April 63 CE

PART II: SARAH'S DIARY

CODEX I: THE GOSPEL OF TRUTH

The Living Book is Revealed

In their hearts the living book of the living was revealed, the book that was written in the Father's thought and mind and was, since the foundation of the All, in his incomprehensible nature. No one had been able to take up this book, since it was ordained that the one who would take it up would be slain. And nothing could appear among those who believed in salvation unless that book had come out.

For this reason the merciful, faithful Jesus was patient and accepted his suffering to the point of taking up that book, since he knew that his death would be life for many...

Jesus appeared,
put on that book,
was nailed to a tree,
and published the Father's edict on the cross.
Oh, what a great teaching!
He humbled himself even unto death,
though clothed in eternal life.
He stripped off the perishable rags
and clothed himself in incorruptibility,
which no one can take from him.

CHAPTER XVI

May 61 CE: Marseille, France

Nero had become Roman emperor in 54 CE and did not conceal his hatred of both Jews and the early Christians. As Bishop of Marseille, Lazarus was a fine prize and would help to deter any future conversions to Christianity. Or so he thought.

Uncle Lazarus was captured and imprisoned in Marseille. Julius was unable to save him - in 40 CE Caligula had ordered the execution of his own father Lucius, a proctor, for refusing to prosecute Caligula's second cousin.

Lazarus was beheaded in May 61 CE and his body was transferred to Autun in eastern France. A distance of some 310 miles from Marseille, his followers thought it would be easier to protect his remains from desecration by the barbarians. Lazarus' sister, Martha wanted to come and pay her respects, but she was dissuaded on grounds of safety, so she remained in her nunnery in Tarascon with her faithful maid Martilla.

Mother, his other sister, remained in La Baume cave, unsurprisingly. At least she was safe there. I visited her to relay the sad tidings, and she didn't look surprised. She already knew of course. Yeshua had taken him to the light; Mother had witnessed this and seen the look of joy on his face. His work was done. Mother handed me a letter addressed to the head librarian of the Serapeum together with her diary - an account of her life since the death of Father. Clearly, she felt her life was drawing to an end also.

Of my original extended family who came with us to Gaul, only Mother, Martha, Martilla and Maximin were still alive, but that would soon change. And no one knew what Nero might do next.

5 April 63 CE: Aix, Provence

Maximin invited me and my two daughters to stay the night before the appointed day that Mother would visit his church for her ascension. He followed the instructions given to him the year before by the priest who visited Mother in La Baume cave. Hurrying to his church in Aix for early morning matins, he went alone into the church and saw Mother amidst the choir of angels who had brought her there. She was raised a distance of some three feet above the floor, standing amongst the angels and lifting her hands in prayer to our Lord. Maximin hesitated to approach her so she turned, and said to him,

"Come closer, father, and do not back away from your daughter."

As he drew near to her, Mother's countenance was so radiant, due to her continuous and daily vision of the angels, that it would have been easier to look directly at the sun than gaze upon her face.

Maximin sent one of his clergy to fetch me and the children, and so together with all the clergy, including the priest who had visited her in her cave; we witnessed Mother, whilst shedding tears of joy, receiving the Lord's body and blood from the Bishop. Then she lay down full length before the steps of the altar, and her holy soul ascended to our Lord. After she expired, so powerful an odour of sweetness pervaded the church that for seven days all those who entered there noticed it. Maximin embalmed her holy body with aromatic lotions and gave her the most honourable burial, giving orders that after his death he was to be buried close to her.

Maximin died peacefully in his sleep, just four weeks later aged 81 years. He was truly devoted to Mother, and was buried as he requested, alongside her.

9th August 63 CE: Birth of Judas

There was great joy in our house when our son was born - little Mary and Anne were so delighted to have a younger brother. Of course, Jean Claude was thrilled on two accounts; he would have a son to carry on his business, and he also looked the image of him, with jet black hair and melted chocolate brown eyes. We named him Judas, after Mother's favourite apostle, who was much maligned and murdered by his fellow apostles.

Mother came to me in a dream and said I should return to Alexandria as soon as I felt fit enough to travel. Jean Claude's business was thriving but Mother had prepared him for this eventuality when he had asked for my hand in marriage.

We were happy in Saintes Maries-de-la-Mer, but I had read Mother's diary and it was clear she wanted me to continue her writing. An education for the children in Alexandria was part of the grand plan. She also had plans for me; she wanted me to attend the Mystery School in Alexandria she had spent time at before she met Father. She called it the 'University of the Soul' and said it was necessary for me to be able to carry on her work. I was both intrigued and excited. I also knew better than to question!

CODEX I: THE TRIPARTITE TRACTATE

Baptism

As for the true baptism, into which the members of the All descend and where they come into being, there is no other baptism except the one - and that is the redemption - which takes place in God the Father, the Son and the Holy Spirit, after confession of faith has been made in those names - which are the single name of the good tidings - and after one has believed that the things one has been told are real.

And on account of this, whoever believes in their reality will obtain salvation, and that means to attain, in an invisible way, the Father, the Son and the Holy Spirit, but only after one has borne witness to them in unfaltering faith and if one grasps them in a firm hope...

The baptism we have spoken about is called **'the garment'** *that is not taken off by the ones who have put it on and that is worn by the ones who have received redemption. It is called* **'the confirmation of truth'**, *which never fails in its constancy and stability and holds fast those who have obtained restoration while they hold onto it. It is called* **'silence'** *because of its tranquillity and unshakeability. It is also called* **'the bridal chamber'** *because of the concord and the inseparability of the ones he has known and who have known him. It is also called* **'the unsinking and fireless light'**, *not because it sheds light, but rather because those who wear it, and who are worn by it as well, are made into light. It is also called* **'the eternal life'**, *which means immortality. Thus it is called...in a manner that is simple, authentic, indivisible, irreducible, complete and unchangeable. For how else can it be named except by referring to it as the ALL? ...It transcends all words, transcends all voice, transcends all mind, transcends all things, and transcends all silence. This is how it is with the things that belong to what it is. This is what it in fact is, with an ineffable and inconceivable character in order to be in those who have knowledge by means of what they have attained, which is that to which they have given glory.*

CHAPTER XVII

16th October 63 CE: Alexandria

Judas was just two months old when we left Marseille. Little Mary aged 5, and Anne aged 4, were overcome with the excitement of going on a long voyage, just as I had been when we left Alexandria all those years ago. Jean Claude put on a brave face; he must have had reservations, but made every effort to conceal them. Travelling was in my bones, since before I was born when Mother fled Judea, sailing to Rome aged one year, and then to Marseille when I was nine. Jean Claude had never left his homeland, so it would be quite a challenge for him.

Julius once again organized a ship and provisions, and insisted on escorting us with two of his favoured guards. Domitia and the children came to the quay for a tearful farewell. Apart from Aunt Martha, who I never saw, they were my only 'family' left in Gaul.

All in all I was happy to return to Alexandria - I was born there after all. Just as well since I had received orders from above! I had a family now and had to think about the future of our children - the education system was far superior to that in Gaul; one of the best in the world. I was hopeful I would be able to enrol them all into the Serapeum, but that was sometime ahead.

My heart skipped a beat when I spotted Pharos lighthouse and I eagerly pointed it out to the children. We had enjoyed good weather, travelling in relative luxury compared to our first voyage in the *'Bark of Mary'*! As we got closer, the lighthouse loomed above us from such a great height that the girls just sat there speechless with their mouths open! As mother had relayed to me all those years ago, I explained to them that it was, unsurprisingly, one of the seven wonders of the ancient world.

And then it hit me - there would be no Philo to greet us. All my memories of growing up at Lake Mareotis were with Philo. When I was in Gaul, I could push it to the back of my mind - I was busy either with Jean Claude's business or with the children, but arriving back in Alexandria it all came flooding back. The finality of not seeing someone again, ever, made my heart ache.

Julius was obliged to stay with the Roman prefect, Gaius Caecina Tuscus and he invited us to stay there also, knowing we had not yet arranged lodgings. Now Julius' residence in Marseille was quite something, but it bore no comparison to this palace in Alexandria! Little Mary and Anne's eyes were out on stalks - the look on their faces was a sight to behold! They felt like princesses and were a little disappointed to find out this would not be our permanent home! Meanwhile, Jean Claude was eager to find premises for his business and rented accommodation for ourselves. He did not feel comfortable in these opulent surroundings; I was in complete agreement with him on this, but did not wish to appear ungrateful or discourteous to our host.

Julius was anxious to return to Marseille while the weather was fair, and regretfully we said goodbye to him. He refused to promise to visit, so I knew in my heart that I would not see him again. He had been like a father to me; I embraced him and thanked him for everything he had done for our family. He shook his head, saying his life would not have been worth living had it not been for meeting Mother, the debt was all his. He certainly restored my faith in human nature. Romans that is; there was good and bad in all of us but I could not see any bad in this man. Truly one of our Lord's servants. What a privilege to have known him..

Gaius said we could stay as long as we wished but I was keen to find somewhere once Julius made his leave. Ideally we would have gone to live at Lake Mareotis, but as it was an adult only community it was out of the question - I was the only child who had ever lived there - they had made an exception for me as I was born there (to the founder no less!).

I wondered if Benjamin and Photini would still be in the house we stayed in all those years ago - I did not remember it of course as Mother was pregnant with me, but she had told me all about their time there and described it in great detail to me. I found it without any difficulty and knocked on the door.

A middle aged woman opened the door and hastened to fetch her employer. I wondered if this was Photini. Benjamin knew who I was instantly, he said I was just as beautiful as my mother, he was overjoyed and insisted we come and stay at once! Benjamin must have been at least 80 years old, but still had great vitality. Photini had looked after him very well indeed! I explained that we had three small children and we would not be the quietest of guests, but he just waved his hands dismissively and said they would give the place some life!

And so we moved into Benjamin's house. He helped Jean Claude find premises for his business and he quickly found work - his style was different to the local workmanship, of top quality, and people were always looking for something different. He also came highly recommended, by Benjamin of course!

We were very happy there. Jean Claude helped with repairs to the house in exchange for a reduced rent until he established himself, which he quickly did. Photini helped mind the children whilst I helped Jean Claude in his shop. The girls loved Alexandria! We shielded them from the less savoury aspects as they were so young, all they saw were the opulent buildings, the zoo, the gardens, the markets - so exciting compared to our little village Saintes Maries-de-la-Mer where they were born. The zoo and the market were their favourite outings; the zoo was home to a wide range of creatures; hippopotami, crocodiles, camels, leopard, lion, monkeys, reptiles and a whole host of brightly coloured birds! Feeding times aroused a cacophony of noise and excitement, much to the girls' amusement! The market's main attraction were the ladies accessories; wigs, jewellery and makeup! The Egyptian women used kohl to decorate their eyes in a most dramatic fashion. I never bought any of course, despite imploring cries from my young daughters, as I never wore makeup. They loved to look though, and I saw no harm in that. They could make their own choices when they were older.

And so for the next three years I dedicated myself to my family; Jean Claude needed my help with his business and I wanted to be there for our children. Looking back, I was never my mother's priority; I was always looked after by someone else and I didn't want my children to have a similar experience. Anyway, I had three of them - there was plenty to do, even with Photini's extra pair of hands!

Jean Claude worked long hours and it paid off - his business flourished. We were able to move into our own home within twelve months. Benjamin was heartbroken - he loved having the children around and the feeling was mutual - they saw him as a fun, playful grandfather who always had time for them. I said we were moving less than a mile away, not back to Gaul - we would still see lots of them! Benjamin understood when I said we wanted our own place, with a garden for the children to play in without being supervised. Photini divided her time between the two houses so there was no disruption for the children. Sadly, Benjamin died within six months of us moving out - the children were understandably upset, but he was 82 years old and had had a good life, enriched by them! Of course, Photini did not hesitate when we asked her to move in with us.

In Alexandria, children start kindergarten school aged seven but it was not available for all and certainly not all girls went to school. If you were a poor child, your chances of being educated were slim, but for a *girl* from a poor background, they were next to zero. For those, their education came from their mothers and fathers. For boys, they learned the family trade. So in Judas' case, he would be apprenticed to Jean Claude as a trainee cabinet maker. For girls, they learned the household responsibilities including cooking, sewing, and taking care of the family business. If a boy was instructed in the art of building or sculpture, his father would hope that his talent was exceptional enough for him to be accepted as a tomb-builder. If a boy failed to learn his trade well, he would be sent out of the city and would have to set up his life in another place.

Historically, in the royal families, girls received equal education to the boys and they often became advisors to the pharaohs. In fact, it was thought that the women had the most influence over major decisions made by the pharaohs. This meant the women had to be versed in politics, philosophy, history, the class writings, mathematics and all of the arts.

And so children of royal families, high officials and nobles had the opportunity to attend the Prince's school. It was also open to boys who showed great promise. This school taught reading and writing, the hieroglyphs, history, mathematics, geometry, geography, cartography, science, ceremonial dance and music, astronomy, astrology, herbal medicine, medicine and religious training.

This was the curriculum I wanted for my children - to receive a formal education supplemented by myself. All residents of Alexandria had unlimited access to thousands of books at the Serapeum. It would be a sacrilege to waste such a valuable resource!

Some schools were designed for specific talents, such as 'Scribes'. These were the people who were entrusted to record all of history, letters and communications. Scribe students would spend hours writing and re-writing the hundreds of symbols that made up the Egyptian language. This could be quite tedious, and children were known to shy away from these studies; those caught playing truant were punished severely.

We were not poor, but we were Jews, therefore not *citizens* and entry to the Serapeum would be difficult. For the sake of my children, I would swim to Marseille and back, so I wrote to Julius and asked him to petition the Roman prefect, Gaius, whom we had stayed with on our arrival. I was asking for all three children to be allowed entry to the highly esteemed Serapeum. We were not looking for charity; we were prepared to pay, and I eagerly awaited his response.

It was some time before Gaius replied; they were prepared to make an exception and admit Judas when he was seven years old. As mere girls, Mary and Anne were not considered eligible.

I was incensed! I marched around to the Roman prefect's residence with all three children in tow and requested an urgent audience with Gaius. Fortunately, the staff recognized us or I doubt they would have granted entry to a half crazed mother with her offspring! This was important to me and the gloves were off. I only had one opportunity to petition him. Metaphorically I threw everything at him. I tried pleading and begging and he remained unmoved. He did not even succumb to flattery and divine threats. I stamped my feet but he just stared back at me; I had to admit I was fighting a losing battle and thought I had better retreat before I lost favour altogether and he changed his mind about Judas. I collected myself and left; this was not the end for me - just a minor setback. I smiled to myself as I thought of Philo - he said no man could ever refuse me when I really wanted something...I would find a way...

Divine intervention would come in the form of a change of prefect the following year, and the appointment of Tiberius Julius Alexander. He was the son of Philo's elder brother Alexander; so my dear Philo had sent his nephew to solve my dilemma! Philo had spoken of him often, sometimes disapprovingly over him placing the interests of the Empire above the Jewish religion, but they had remained on good terms. Philo taught me it was best to avoid falling out with people - most disagreements were through lack of communication and could be solved peacefully. It often took longer, but allowing people to 'save face' meant their dignity and self-respect could remain intact and a door could be kept ajar, if not open. He was so right. I thought of his words as I wrote to Tiberius requesting an audience. I was delighted when I was granted one almost immediately; we got along famously, and we talked mainly of my times with Philo, who had clearly spoken of me both favourably and fondly. He said he knew of course why I had come to see him and was happy to grant the girls an education at the Serapeum! Politically I could see it would also be good for his reputation in the Jewish community.

This was one of the happiest days of my life! My legacy to them would be the education of mind, body and soul - they were an important bloodline and responsibilities would come with this in the future.

Mary and Anne started at kindergarten at the famed Serapeum in September 66 CE. They were taught reading, writing and mathematics. Their lessons were in Greek and Egyptian; at home Jean-Claude spoke to them in Gallic, and I in Hebrew, as my mother had done with me. They kept themselves to themselves, although the novelty of being the only girls quickly wore off and they earned respect from their classmates.

Judas missed them terribly at first, but was spoilt rotten by Photini! When we weren't on outings to the zoo or the gardens, he would 'help' her with the cleaning so it would take three times as long - but they had so much fun!

So now it was time for me to keep my promise to Mother and make contact with the Mystery School of Akhenaten. I made an appointment to see the Head Librarian saying I had a letter to deliver personally to her. I was greeted by one of her deputies who gave me a long stare before scurrying into a back room for some minutes. An elderly Egyptian woman with an inscrutable face appeared, and I handed her the letter. Her wizened face broke into a broad smile as she told me she remembered Mother and they had been waiting for me. She said they would like to start as soon as possible and so my education began the following day! After leaving Judas with Photini, I would drop the girls off at the main entrance, cover my head and face with a shawl, and make my way to the rear of the building where a stairway led to the catacombs under the main building. A password granted access; *"Know thyself and be free!"*, although there were several and they changed frequently.

The information the elders shared with me was simply unbelievable. I was sworn to secrecy of course, I could not even tell Jean Claude or Photini of my whereabouts. As part of my mission, I was given permission to reveal some of the information together with my diary, which would be discovered many years later.

Now I understood why Mother wanted me to return to Alexandria - it was all part of the divine plan...

The following are just some of the mysteries revealed to me..

The Ancient Egyptians were obsessed with immortality and the migration of souls. The preservation of information, both in the mystery schools and mummification process, ascension and resurrection. There was meticulous preparation for the after-life. They believed that if they understood the creation process and the mechanics of the universe, they would achieve immortality. A number of them did..

The Flower of Life

The Flower of Life belongs to sacred geometry which believes that all life is  part of a divine, geometric plan. From the invisible atom to the stars in our galaxy. It consists of 19 overlapping circles and interconnecting circles. Always 19, no more, no less... The Flower of Life is the primal language of the universe, pure shape and proportion. It reveals the harmonic energy patterns by which nature creates and designs. These geometric codes show parallels between patterns in flowers, snowflakes, shells and even the stars in our galaxy. Looking at the symbol has an emotional effect on the observer, whether they are conscious of it or not. It affects our soul.

It is called a flower because it represents the cycle of a fruit tree. The fruit tree makes a flower, which turns into a fruit; the fruit contains a seed, which falls to the ground, then grows into another tree. Just five miraculous steps represent the cycle of life. The Flower of Life symbol is found on temple and pyramid walls; for example, inside the Temple of Osiris in Abydos and under the Great Pyramid. These buildings were constructed with utter precision and harmony.

The Flower of Life carries a hidden message and by joining up intersecting lines one finds the Metatrons' Cube.

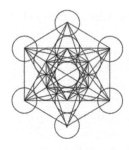

Metatron's Cube

Metatron's Cube contains all the platonic solids that exist in the universe; the tetrahedron, cube, octahedron, dodecahedron and icosahedron. All sides and angles of a platonic solid are equal. They are known as platonic solids because Plato linked them to the spirit world of heaven and the physical elements on earth.

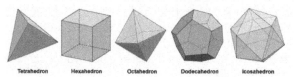

Tetrahedron   Hexahedron   Octahedron   Dodecahedron   Icosahedron

Above: Platonic solids

Merkaba

The Merkaba is a counter-rotating field of light surrounding our bodies for approximately 55-60 feet. It affects spirit and body simultaneously and can be used as an interdimensional vehicle. The *Mer* (counter-rotating field of light) - *ka* (spirit) - *ba* (body), also known as "Chariot" or "Throne of God" requires activation, but this only needs to be done once. The Merkaba contains all your knowledge and wisdom and can transport your spirit anywhere. If you travel in your Merkaba body you shrink to the size of an orb!

Star tetrahedron, or a 3 dimensional Star of David

It comprises two tetrahedrons; the male or sun one (facing up - top) spins anti-clockwise at a ratio of 34 to the female or earth tetrahedron (point facing down - bottom) which spins at a ratio of 21 (34:21).

In addition to intention and specific breathing patterns the Merkaba can only be activated with divine, unconditional love, when one is connected to the sacred space in one's heart. One needs to feed and then nourish the Merkaba with love and die consciously to avoid reincarnation.

What the Ancients were looking to achieve was possible with the

Merkaba. If you are aware of your Merkaba and 'die' consciously, you pass into the next dimension, circumventing the resurrection process where you are reborn into a new body. So when a person ascends, he or she simply disappears from this dimension and appears in the next!

Yeshua referred to the Merkaba near the end of *The Secret Book of James* with the words,

"I shall depart from you, for the chariot of spirit has carried me up.."

The Great Pyramid and Sphinx

Below the Great Pyramid, there are 48 images etched on a single wall. The first symbol is the Flower of Life. The next 47 images are all connected with the ascension process. This is the fundamental purpose of the Great Pyramid - resurrection and ascension.

The Sphinx is the largest sculpture on earth, around 50,000 years old. One mile under the Sphinx, inside a large round room, lies the oldest synthetic object in the world. Several hundred feet across, disk shaped, and flat on the top and bottom. Its skin is so thin it is transparent. It is a ship connected directly to the spirit of Mother Earth, a protector of our planet. It is propelled by thoughts and feelings.

Throughout the course of our history, unbeknown to most of us, there have been threats to our planet from life forms from other planets. Fortunately, someone on Earth with a high consciousness is forewarned of this, locates the ship and raises the vibration of the molecules only one overtone higher than the Earth exists on. This allowed him or her and the ship to rise up through the Earth and into the sky. Mother Earth and the Sun connect within that person and give him or her great power, and whatever that person thinks or feels happens. So that person will think of a scenario to make the problem disappear, so it is a warship without weapons - problems are just 'thought away'! This keeps our evolutionary process going, without any kind of outside unwanted influence. So far, anyway..

Alchemy

Al means God. *Chem* or *Khem* is from *Kimia* (Greek) which means to fuse or cast a metal. *Khem* was the ancient name for Egypt. So alchemy means 'to fuse with God'.

Alchemy is the science and art of causing change, both physically and spiritually. On the material side, it is a process whereby base metals are turned into gold. Metaphorically, gold is spiritual perfection, while the base metals, such as lead, are impure states of the spirit, unenlightened and full of the problems of mortal life.

The ancient Mesopotamians called it *shem-an-na* and we called it *mfkzt*, a white powder made from high-spun gold and platinum. We revered it as a gift from paradise as it was a 'powder of projection' which we put into a conical shaped bread. It produces brilliant light and deadly rays, but more importantly, can induce extraordinary powers of levitation, transmutation and teleportation. It would be later known as the 'philosopher's stone', although it was not a stone at all.

True alchemists were never trying to make a potion for eternal life, or a 'stone' that would transform base metals into gold - it was the process that was key. They saw it as identical to the process of ascension a human follows going from his or her present level of consciousness to the next, or even enlightenment.

Alchemy is the study of how to keep all things in balance. If you understand geometries and know what their relationships are, as in sacred geometry, you will understand the map beneath it all. And this will enable you to understand everything.

So the Ancient Egyptians were extremely advanced, both spiritually and scientifically, and understood about God, creation and the universe...

———————————

I attended the Mystery School for a year, fitting in with the girls' school terms. It was the most challenging yet rewarding part of my education and I will always feel greatly privileged to have received this information I am now sharing with you. I have been guided to stop now, for fear of this information getting into the wrong hands - it has great power and could inflict irreversible harm both on the user and on others if used incorrectly.

CODEX V : THE GOSPEL OF JUDAS

Opening

The secret revelatory discourse that Jesus spoke with Judas Iscariot in the course of a week, three days before his passion.

Jesus Speaks Privately with Judas

Jesus understood that Judas was contemplating the rest of what is lofty, and he said to him,

"Move away from the others, and I shall explain to you the mysteries of the kingdom, not so that you can attain it, as you will go through a great deal of grief. For somebody else will take your place, so that the twelve disciples may be complete once again with their god."...

NB: Although The Gospel of Judas is part of Codex V and from the Nag Hammadi library it was not discovered until the 1970's and first published in 2006.

CHAPTER XVIII

January 66 CE: Jerusalem riots

The Jerusalem riots of 66 CE took place in the centre of Roman Judea, and became the catalyst of the Great Revolt in Judea. The violence began at Caesarea in January 66 CE, provoked by some Greek merchants sacrificing birds in front of a local synagogue. The Roman garrison did not intervene and so the long-standing Greek and Jewish religious tensions were re-ignited.

Protests over taxation joined the list of grievances and random attacks on Roman citizens and perceived 'traitors' occurred in Jerusalem. Tension reached a breaking point when the Roman procurator of Judea, Gessius Florus, sent Roman troops to remove seventeen talents from the Temple treasury, claiming the money was for unpaid taxes.

Some of the Jewish population openly mocked Florus by passing a basket around to collect money as if Florus was poor. Rioters attacked a garrison, killing the soldiers. Florus reacted to the unrest by sending soldiers into Jerusalem the following day to raid the city and arrest a number of the leaders. These were later whipped and crucified, despite many of them being Roman citizens.

Outraged Judean nationalist factions took up arms and the Roman military garrison of Jerusalem was quickly overrun by rebels. In September 66, the Romans in Jerusalem surrendered and were lynched. At the same time, the Greek inhabitants of the capital of Judea, Caesarea, attacked their Jewish neighbours; the Jews replied by expelling many Greeks from Judea, Galilee and the Golan heights. Fearing for his own life, the pro-Roman king Agrippa II and his sister Berenice fled Jerusalem to Galilee. Judean militias later rose up against Roman citizens of Judea and those with Roman sympathies, cleansing the country of any Roman symbols.

February 67 CE, Tarascon, France: Martha ascends

Julius forwarded a letter from Martha's faithful servant, Martilla, advising me that Aunt Martha had passed on to celestial spheres in February 67 CE. She was 58 years old.

Martilla related that during the year before her death, our Lord revealed to Martha the time of her passing. Throughout that year she suffered continually from fevers. Then a week before she died, she heard the angelic choirs bearing her sister Mary's soul to heaven. She called all her brothers and sisters in religion together and said,

"My companions and dear friends, rejoice with me, I beg of you, because I rejoice at the sight of the choirs of angels bearing my sister Mary's soul to the promised mansions! O my beautiful and beloved sister, may you live in the blessed abode with him who was your master and my guest!"

At that very moment Martha sensed the nearness of her death, and cautioned her companions to keep the lamps lit and to watch over her until she died. However, at midnight the day before her passing, when those watching her had fallen asleep, a strong wind blew through and blew out all the lamps. She was aware of a swarm of evil spirits surrounding her and began to pray,

"Lord Jesus, my dear Guest! My seducers, holding lists of all the wrongs I have done, are gathered here to devour me! Lord Jesus, do not abandon me!"

Then she saw her sister Mary coming towards her, carrying a torch with which she lit all the candles and lamps, and Jesus Christ appeared, saying,

"Come, beloved hostess, and where I am, you will be with me! You welcomed me into your house, I shall welcome you into my heaven, and for the love of you I shall listen favourably to those who invoke you!".

As the hour of her death approached, she had herself carried outside so that she might see the heavens, and asked that she be laid down upon the earth and a cross be held before her eyes. Then she prayed the following words,

"My dear Guest, take care of your poor little servant, and, as you deigned to accept my hospitality, receive me now into your heavenly dwelling!"

Then Martha asked to have the gospel according to Luke read to her, and at the words, "Father, into thy hands I commend my spirit", she inhaled her last breath.

On the following day, which was a Sunday, the office of lauds was being chanted around Martha's body, while in Perigrueux, at the third hour, Bishop Fronto was celebrating a solemn mass. At the reading of the epistle he fell asleep, and the Lord appeared to him and said,

"My beloved Fronto, if you want to fulfil the promise you once made to our hostess, rise quickly and follow me!".

Immediately they were in Tarascon and led the singing around Martha's body as they proceeded to lay her body in a tomb. Meanwhile, in Perigueux, the Deacon, who was about to chant the gospel, awoke Bishop Fronto to ask his blessing. Fronto, barely awake, answered,

"My brothers, why did you awaken me? Our Lord Jesus Christ brought me to the body of Martha his hostess and we carried her to her burial! Quick, send messengers to bring my gold ring and silver gloves. I entrusted them to the sacristan as I prepared to bury her, and forgot to retrieve them as you awoke me so suddenly!"

The messengers found the items as the Bishop had said, and brought back the ring but only one glove; the sacristan kept the other glove in memory of the event.

Fronto recalled that as they were leaving the church after Martha's burial, a brother from that place, who was learned in letters, followed and asked the Bishop what his name was. The Bishop said nothing but showed the brother an open book he was carrying in his hand, on which was written nothing, save the following verse;

"In perpetual memory; my hostess will be just, she will not be afraid of hearing evil on the last day".

When the brother inspected the book further, he found the same verse was written on every page.

Martilla ended her letter by saying she no longer wished to remain in Tarascon without Martha and would be travelling to Slovania to preach the gospel there. She lived happily there until she died in her sleep ten years later in 77 CE. She had requested that after her death her body should be returned to Tarascon where she could be laid to rest near her beloved

Martha. This was duly carried out by her followers.

Many miracles would take place at Martha's tomb. Clovis, king of the Franks, had become a Christian after being baptized by Remy. Suffering from a serious kidney disease, he went to Martha's tomb and prayed for his health to be restored. He fully recovered, and in return for this favour, he endowed land, including strongholds and villas, for three miles around on both banks of the Rhone, declaring the area free of taxes in perpetuity.

Martha was the last of my surviving family in Gaul. None of my family feared death, for Mother I am sure she had been longing to be reunited with Father, but for those of us left behind, it can be most unsettling.

Apart from Julius and his family, there was no one there I was close to. There really was nothing to go back for; my family's future was in Alexandria, and when my children's education was complete we would return to Lake Mareotis to fulfil Mother's wishes.

April 68 CE, Alexandria: the martyrdom of Mark

I had been concerned for the safety of Mark for some time, but he refused to heed my advice and leave the city. He would merely reply, "What is the point of fleeing from one's persecutors? I am not frightened of them!". I tried to argue that he was of more use to our Lord alive than dead, but my words fell on stony ground. Surely it is how we lived our lives, not how we died that matters? Loving unconditionally, showing patience and devotional discipline may inspire a fellow seeker's path to enlightenment. Surely that is more fruitful than being worshipped as a saint, as many martyrs become?

So whilst Mark was celebrating mass on Easter Sunday in 68 CE near the end of Nero's reign, the priests of the temple assembled in the church and put a rope around his neck, and dragged him through the city, shouting,

"Let's haul the wild ox to the slaughterhouse!". They scourged his body; scraps of his flesh were strewn on the road and the stones became blood stained. They shut him up in jail in solitary confinement but an angel came to comfort him. Our Lord also appeared to give him courage, saying,

"Mark, my evangelist, fear not! I am with you to deliver you!". When morning came, they once again put a rope around his neck and dragged him around the streets of the city to put fear into the Christians calling out,

"Haul the wild ox to the shambles!" As Mark was dragged along, he gave thanks, saying,

"Into your hands, O Lord, I commend my spirit," and with these words he expired.

The pagans wanted to burn his body, but suddenly the air was turbulent, hail drummed down, lightning flashed, and everyone rushed to find shelter, so they left Mark's body untouched. Some of his followers quickly took his body away and buried him with great reverence inside the church he had founded.

CODEX V : THE GOSPEL OF JUDAS

Jesus Appears to the Disciples Again

The next day, in the morning, he appeared to his disciples. They said to him, "Master, where did you go and what did you do when you departed from us?" Jesus said to them, "I went to a different generation, one that is great and holy." His disciples said to him, "Master, what is the great generation that is exalted over us and is holy, but is not present in these realms?"... Jesus... laughed and said to them, "Why are you reflecting in your minds about the generation that is powerful and holy? I tell you the truth, no one born of this realm will behold that generation, no angelic host of the stars will rule over that generation, no human of mortal birth will be able to accompany it, because that generation is not from... that has come to be... The generation of people among you is from the generation of humanity... power, which... powers... through which you rule."

When his disciples heard these things, each one was troubled in spirit. They were speechless.

Judas Asks About His Own Fate

Jesus said to him, "... you will go through a great deal of grief when you see the kingdom and its entire generation."

When Judas heard this he said, "What advantage is there for me, since you have set me apart from that generation?"

*Jesus answered and said, **"You will be the thirteenth, and you will be cursed by the other generations, but eventually you will rule over them."***

CHAPTER XIX

September 69 CE: Assault on Jonapata

The Romans' first assault was in Jonapata, where Josephus was both scribe and ruler, and he and his people put up a brave resistance. But Josephus, seeing that the city's fall was inevitable, took eleven Jews with him and sought refuge in an underground room.

After four days without food, his associates, though Josephus disagreed, preferred to die rather than submit to servitude under the Romans. They wanted to kill each other and offer their blood in sacrifice to God. Josephus, being a prudent man and not wishing to die, appointed himself arbiter of death and sacrifice, and ordered the others to cast lots, and ordered the others to cast lots, two by two, to determine which of the pair would put the other to death. The lots were cast and one man after the other was consigned to death, until the last one was left to draw lots with Josephus. Then Josephus, who was a strong agile man, took the other man's sword away from him and asked him which he preferred, life or death, ordering him not to waste time choosing. The man, afraid, answered,

"I do not refuse to live, if by your favour I am able to save your life." And so his life ended there and then.

Josephus thought his only hope of survival was through wile rather than force. He had a talk in hiding with one of Vespasian's aides, who Josephus was on friendly terms with. He requested an audience with Vespasian with the intention of asking for his life to be spared, and that his request was granted. He was taken before Vespasian, who said to him,

"You would have deserved death, if this man's petition had not secured your freedom!"

Josephus replied, "If anything wrong has been done, it can be set right!"

Vespasian was unconvinced: "What can a conquered man do?"

Josephus answered, "I will be able to do something, if what I say wins me a favourable hearing."

"It is granted that you may say what you have to say, and if there is any good in it, you will be listened to quietly."

Josephus played his trump card and announced with great authority, "The Roman emperor has died, and the Senate has made you emperor!"

Vespasian was delighted at this but remained unconvinced, after all he was hearing it from a man trying to save his life. He questioned him further,

"If you are a prophet, why did you not prophesy to this city that it was about to fall under my sway?"

Josephus was quick to respond, "I foretold it publicly for forty days!".

Shortly thereafter legates arrived from Rome, affirming that Vespasian had indeed been elevated to the imperial throne, and took him off to Rome.

Titus, son of Vespasian, on hearing of his father's accession to the empire, was so filled with joy and exultation that he caught a chill and suffered a contraction of nerves and muscles that left him painfully paralyzed in one leg.

Josephus heard that Titus was paralyzed, and diligently sought information on the nature and timing of his affliction. The cause was unknown, as was the nature of the illness, but the time was known. It happened to Titus when he learned of his father's election. Josephus, quick of mind and foresighted, put two and two together and surmised both the nature of the ailment and its cure. He knew that Titus had been debilitated by an excess of joy and gladness, and bearing in mind that opposites are often cured by opposites, and what is brought on by love is often dispelled by dislike, Josephus enquired if there was anyone the Emperor's son found particularly obnoxious. There was a slave who annoyed Titus so much the very sight of him, even the mention of his name, incensed him beyond all reason. So Josephus said to Titus,

"If you want to be cured, guarantee the safety of any who come in my company."

Titus immediately replied, "Whoever comes in your company will be safe!".

Josephus promptly arranged a festive dinner, set his own table facing that of Titus, and seated the slave at his right side. When Titus saw the slave, he growled with immense displeasure; as he had been chilled by joy, he was now heated by a fit of fury. His sinews were loosened, and he was cured. Thereafter Titus granted his favour to the slave and became friends with Josephus.

February - September 70 CE; The Siege of Jerusalem

We believed the destruction of Jerusalem to be a punishment for the death of our Lord. But because our Lord did not wish the death of a sinner, he gave them almost forty years to do penance, and called upon them through the apostles, and especially through James the brother of our Lord, who continually preached repentance among them. When this proved futile, God willed to terrify them with wonders. There were many prodigies and portents, but none were heeded. An extraordinarily brilliant star, similar in shape to a sword, hung over the city of Jerusalem for a year, shooting out flames.

On a certain feast of Unleavened Bread, at the ninth hour of the night, a light shone around the altar of the Temple, so brilliant that all present thought a marvellously bright day had dawned. At the same feast a heifer that was in the hands of the priests to be sacrificed, gave birth to a lamb. Some days later, at the hour of sunset, cars and chariots were seen racing across every quarter of the sky, with battalions of armed men clashing in the clouds surrounding the city with troops.

Four years before the war, at the feast of Tabernacles, a man named Jesus, son of Ananias, suddenly began to shout,

"A voice from the East, a voice from the West, a voice from the four winds, a voice over Jerusalem and over the Temple, a voice over husbands and wives, a voice over the whole people!".

The man was caught, beaten and whipped, but the more he was whipped, the louder he shouted. He was brought before the judge and tortured but neither begged nor wept, just repeated the same words, adding, "Woe, woe to Jerusalem!".

Previously, when Pontius Pilate realised he had condemned an innocent man and feared the displeasure of Tiberius Caesar, he sent an envoy named Albanus to present his excuses to the emperor. But Pilate's envoy was driven ashore in Galatia (Turkey) by unfavourable winds and taken to Vespasian, who at that time was governor of Galatia. The custom in Galatia at that time was that anyone who had been shipwrecked had to give his goods and services to the ruler. So Vespasian asked Albanus who he was, where he came from and where he was going. Albanus answered,

"I come from Jerusalem and I was on my way to Rome."

Vespasian replied excitedly, "You come from the land of the wise men, you know the art of medicine, you are a physician! You must cure me!"

Since childhood he had been afflicted with some kind of worms in his nose, hence his name Vespasian. Albanus contested,

"My lord, I know nothing of medicine and am therefore unable to cure you!"

"Cure me or die!" Vespasian shouted in desperation.

Albanus calmly responded, "He who gave sight to the blind, drove out spirits, and raised the dead, knows I have no knowledge of healing."

This aroused Vespasian's curiosity and he enquired,

"Who is this that you say such great things about?"

"Jesus of Nazareth, whom the Jews, in their envy, put to death! If you believe in him you will obtain the grace of health."

Vespasian immediately replied, "I believe, I believe, because he who raised the dead will be able to free me of this ailment!"

As he said this, the worms fell out of his nose and he received his health then and there. Filled with joy, he said,

"I am sure that he who was able to cure me is the Son of God. I will seek permission from the emperor, go with an armed band to Jerusalem, and overthrow all those who betrayed and killed this man!"

He turned to Albanus and said,

"Your life and goods are safe and unharmed, and you have my permission to return home."

Vespasian then went to Rome and obtained Tiberius Caesar's permission to destroy Jerusalem and Judea. For years he built up several armies, not openly acting out of zeal for Christ, but under the pretext of defending the Roman Empire from the Jews who were rebelling.

And so our Lord brought Vespasian and Titus to Jerusalem, razing the city to its foundations. Some time before their arrival, the Christian faithful who were in Jerusalem had been warned by the Holy Spirit to leave the city, and to take refuge in a town called Pella, across the Jordan. Thus with all her holy men withdrawn, the vengeance of heaven fell upon Jerusalem.

Vespasian put his son Titus in charge of the Roman army, with Tiberius Julius Alexander as his second-in command; they besieged and conquered the city of Jerusalem, which had been controlled by Judean rebel factions since 66 CE, when the Judean Free Government was formed in Jerusalem in response to the riots in 66 CE.

The siege ended on 30 August 70 CE with the burning and destruction of its Second Temple, and the Romans entered and sacked the Lower City. The destruction of both the first and second temples would be mourned annually with the Jewish fast Tisha B'Av. Titus commissioned and had built the Arch of Titus to celebrate the Roman ransack of Jerusalem and the Temple. The conquest of Jerusalem was complete on 8 September 70 CE.

Despite early success in repelling Roman sieges, the Zealots fought amongst themselves and lacked proper leadership, resulting in poor discipline, training and ill preparation for the battles which were to follow. At one point they destroyed the food stocks in the city, a misguided measure thought to have been taken in order to enlist a merciful God's intervention on behalf of the besieged Jews, or as a means of making the defenders more determined, and more able to resist the Roman army.

Titus began his siege a few days before Passover, and Jerusalem was full of many people who had come to celebrate the festival. The initial thrust of the siege began at the Third Wall, north of the Jaffa Gate. By May this was breached, and the Second Wall taken shortly afterwards, leaving the defenders in possession of the Temple and the upper and lower city. The Roman siege engineers erected ramparts and then had a wall built to surround the city in order to starve out the population more effectively. After several failed attempts to breach or scale the walls of the Fortress of Antonia, the Romans finally launched a secret attack, overcoming the sleeping Zealots and taking the fortress by late July.

After Jewish allies killed a number of Roman soldiers, Titus sent his Jewish friend Josephus to negotiate with the defenders; this ended with Jews wounding the Jewish negotiator with an arrow, and another sally was launched soon after. Titus was almost captured during this sudden attack, but managed to escape.

Overlooking the Temple compound, the fortress provided a perfect point from which to attack the Temple itself. Battering rams made little progress; but a Roman soldier threw a burning stick onto one of the Temple's walls, which set fire and rapidly spread out of control. Destroying the 500 year old Temple was not Titus' aim; he had wanted to seize it and transform it into a temple dedicated to the Roman Emperor and the Roman pantheon. The Temple was captured and destroyed, and the flames spread into the residential areas of the city.

The Roman legions quickly crushed the remaining Jewish resistance. Some of the remaining Jews escaped through hidden underground tunnels and sewers, while others made a final stand in the Upper City. This temporarily halted the Roman advance as they had to construct siege towers to vanquish the remaining Jews. Herod's Palace fell on 7th September, and the city was completely under Roman control by 8th September.

Josephus later recorded that more than one million people were killed during the siege, the majority of which were Jewish. The celebration of Passover meant the number of people in the city was abnormally high - many were visitors who had become entangled in the fighting and unable to escape.

Armed rebels, as well as frail citizens, were sentenced to death. All of Jerusalem's remaining 97,000 citizens became Roman prisoners. Thousands were forced to become gladiators and died in the arena. Others were forced to assist in the building of the Forum of Peace and the Colosseum. Those under 17 years of age were sold into servitude.

Titus and his soldiers celebrated victory upon their return to Rome by parading the Menorah and Table of the Bread of God's Presence through the streets. Up until then, these sacred items had only ever been set eyes on by the high priest of the Temple.

Titus refused to accept a wreath of victory, saying that the victory did not come through his own efforts, and he had merely acted as an instrument of divine wrath.

Many fled to areas around the Mediterranean, including Alexandria; shock waves echoed throughout the Jewish community for years, survivors traumatized and reliving horrific tales of brutality, of the torture of citizens young and old at the hands of the soldiers. It was the greatest massacre of our people and I feared for my family's safety.

CODEX V: THE GOSPEL OF JUDAS

Cosmos, Chaos, Underworld

"Now the multitude of those immortal beings is called 'cosmos', that is, corruption, through the Father and the seventy-two luminaries with the Self-Generated and his seventy-two eternal beings. There the first human appeared, with his incorruptible powers. The eternal being that appeared with his generation, the one in whom are the cloud of knowledge and the angel, is called El...

"After these things he said, 'Let twelve angels come into existence to rule over chaos and the underworld. And look, from the cloud an angel appeared whose face blazed with fire and whose countenance was fouled with blood. His name was Nebro, which is interpreted as 'rebel', but others name him Yaldabaoth. And another angel, Sakla, also came from the cloud. So Nebro created six angels, with Sakla, to be attendants, and these produced twelve angels in the heavens, and each one received a share in the heavens."

Jesus Speaks of Judas's Act of Turning Him In

Jesus said "But you will exceed all of them. For you will sacrifice the man who bears me. Already your horn has been lifted up, and your anger has flared up, and your star has burned brightly, and your heart has grown strong.

"I tell you the truth, your last days...become...grieve...the ruler, since he will be overthrown. And then the generation of the great generation of Adams will be magnified, for before the heaven, the earth, and the angels, that generations from the eternal realms exists.

*"Look, you have been informed of everything. Lift up your eyes and behold the cloud and the light that is within it and the stars that are circling it. **And the star that leads the way is your star.**"*

CHAPTER XX

September 72 CE: Lake Mareotis

Mary was now fourteen years old, Anne thirteen and Judas nine, and they were all weekly boarding at the Serapeum. I thought Judas was too young to board - he had only been at school for two years, but he refused to be left at home with Jean Claude, Photini and myself! They all seemed to realize what an incredible opportunity they had been given and were serious with their studies from day one.

Judas was very sporty, which made him popular with the other boys and provided a healthy balance to his studies. He was already a competent boxer and wrestler and would spar with Jean Claude in their 'play fights'. Mary and Anne were both diligent as well as intelligent and were consistently top of their classes. Mary and Anne signed up for extra-curricular clubs; debating, drama, dance, swimming - there were simply not enough hours in the days for everything they wanted to do! Jean Claude and I were proud parents but were careful not to crow as we were well aware that a special case had been made for our daughters. I prayed all girls would have the same opportunities as boys, before our children had finished their education. It was important they did well - the authorities needed to see that they could be a valuable asset rather than a hindrance to our society.

Once they reached puberty the girls could choose to opt for 'priestess' training, from the Temple of Isis, which is what Mother did when she first came to Alexandria all those years ago. They would carry on with the main curriculum, but widen their studies to include astronomy, astrology, metaphysics, herbal medicine, alchemy, magical arts, calligraphy, design and sculpture. I loved hearing from them about their lectures and practical classes - their tutors were always trying to improve their training without disregarding traditions which had survived thousands of years.

Judas would go to Jean Claude's workshop with him when he had finished his studies. He loved watching his father work; Jean Claude would train him as a cabinet maker so one day, if he chose, he could carry on his business. This was the Jewish way; for the father to pass on his trade to his sons.

Supper times provided an opportunity for them to practice their debating skills on Jean Claude and myself - Photini used to shake her head in disbelief sometimes - it could become quite heated but never ever unpleasant!. I saw them as acorns who would grow into strong oak trees - they would have to withstand storms in their adult lives and the ability to verbally stand their corner was essential. As Philo had continually reminded me, it was important not to fall out with people.

Mother came to me in a dream one night and said I should split my time between the family home and Lake Mareotis; whilst the children were in school I could live at Lake Mareotis during the week and start writing. It was time; Jean Claude had two men working for him as well as a clerk to invoice and collect payments. Jean Claude was put in charge of building maintenance at Lake Mareotis so I saw lots of him. He never charged the community of course - this was his offering.

Photini was there to run the house and I would be home on Friday evenings before the children were. If there was a problem or one of the children was unwell, they took priority. I could be home within a few hours - I was not far away.

If Jean Claude missed me he did not say anything; Mother had made it clear to him before we were married that this would be my future. When the children finished school it was my intention to move the family back to Lake Mareotis; of course the children would have a choice, but their bloodline suggested this was destiny.

And so over the next two years I wrote Codex I: *The Prayer of the Apostle Paul, The Secret Book of James, The Gospel of Truth, The Treatise on the Resurrection and The Tripartite Tractate.*

I took a leaf out of mother's book by assigning the first two tractates to Paul and James respectively. Anonymity was a safer option; for now anyway, the truth would come out eventually, long after I was gone!

I was happy. I had seclusion and purpose in my childhood home at Lake Mareotis - I felt very close to Mother and Philo when I was there. Returning to the chaos and fun of family life with Jean Claude and the children at weekends and school holidays kept me grounded -my family was very important to me.

But nothing lasts forever...

July 76 CE: The stoning of James, son of Alpheus

In the back of my mind I always feared for the apostles' safety, knowing they were in mortal danger every day of their lives. Simon the Zealot, now Bishop of Jerusalem, wrote to me telling me of the execution of James, son of Alpheus.

James had several names; James, son of Alpheus, the brother of our Lord, James the Less, and James the Just. Not only the son of Alpheus, but also by meaning. *Alpheus* is interpreted as learned, or document, or fugitive, or thousandth, because James was 'learned' through inspired knowledge, a 'document' by instructing others, a 'fugitive' from the world because he despised it, and 'thousandth' because of his reputation for humility.

He is called the brother of our Lord as he bore a very strong resemblance to Yeshua; very often they were mistaken for one another. Yeshua asked Judas to point him out as he was one of the few who could distinguish our Lord from James. Ignatius confirms this likeness in his letter to John the Evangelist:

"If I have your permission, I want to come up to Jerusalem to see the venerable James, surnamed the Just, who they say resembled Jesus Christ so closely in his features, his life, and his way with others that he might have been born his twin brother; so that, as they say, if I see James I see Jesus Christ so far as all bodily features are concerned."

James is also called James the Less to distinguish him from James, the son of Zebedee, for James of Zebedee was born before James of Alpheus, and James of Alpheus was called to be an apostle later. In many religious communities it is customary that the one who enters earlier is called the greater, and the one who comes later the less, though the less may be either older, or more holy, or both.

James is called the Just because of the merit of his devout holiness. According to Jerome his holiness was so revered by the people that they strove eagerly to touch the hem of his garment. Hergesippus, wrote in

Ecclesiastical History,

"James, the brother of the Lord, assumed the role of the Church...From his mother's womb he was holy. He drank no wine or strong drink, never ate meat, no razor ever came near his head, no oil anointed him, he never bathed. His clothing consisted of a linen garment. He knelt so often in prayer that his knees were calloused like the soles of his feet. For this endless righteousness he was called the Just and Abba, meaning the stronghold of the people and righteousness".

On Easter Sunday in 40 CE, the apostles had gathered in Jerusalem and James asked how much our Lord had done among the people through them, and so they gave their account. Then for seven days James and the other apostles preached in the Temple before Caiaphas and a number of Jews. Suddenly a man came into the Temple and shouted,

"O men of Israel, what are you doing? Why do you let these sorcerers delude us?"

He stirred up the people so much that they wanted to stone the apostles. The man climbed up to the platform from which James was preaching and threw him to the floor below; as a result James limped badly for the rest of his life.

In July 76 CE, the tyrannical persecution from the Jews was aimed at James. The Jews assembled and said to the people,

"We pray you, call the people back, because they are wrong about Jesus."

"Most righteous of men, to whom we all owe deference, the people are wrong in following Jesus who was crucified! Tell us plainly what you think about him!"

"Why do you question me about the son of Man? Behold, he is seated in the heavens at the right of the sovereign Power, and he will come to judge the living and the dead!"

The Christians rejoiced at hearing this and listened to him gladly. But the Pharisees and the Scribes said to each other,

"We made a mistake in allowing him to give testimony to Jesus! Let us go and throw him down! That will frighten this crowd and they won't dare believe what he has said!"

Then all together, as loudly as they could, they shouted,

"Oh! The just man has erred!" Then they went up, threw him down and began to stone him. But James, though beaten to the ground, raised himself to his knees and said,

"I pray to you Lord, forgive them, for they know not what they do!"

At this, one of the priests, of the sons of Rahab, cried,

"Stop! What are you doing? This man is praying for you!"

But one of the persecutors picked up a club and aimed a heavy blow at James' head, splitting his skull. The Christians were determined to avenge his death and capture and punish the persecutors, but they escaped. So they took James' body and buried him with reverence.

We had a service of thanksgiving for beloved James at Lake Mareotis; he was a most faithful servant of our Lord. His work was done, and he would now be rejoicing, enjoying the company of angels and the raptures of heaven.

I received a letter from Julius in September 77 CE to say he had been appointed Governor of Britain. Although reluctant to uproot his family, this was a promotion and a huge honour; by the time I was reading his letter he and his family would no longer be in Marseille. So my final tie with Gaul was severed; Lake Mareotis was where I was born and where I would spend the rest of my days.

Over the years the family attended most, if not all the major festivals celebrated at Lake Mareotis - they knew everyone in the community and it became a second home to them. In July 81 CE when they had all finished school, it was a natural step for them to move to Lake Mareotis. Each of us would have our own cabin. I told them it was not compulsory and it was not forever - they all had to make their own life choices. It was beyond my wildest dreams what they would do....

Photini was now 72 years old and so she came with us too! She asked one of her young relatives to take over her duties in our home in Alexandria. Photini said she had wanted to move there in the beginning in 33 CE - she joked that it had taken her nearly 50 years to get there. She had also wanted to come to Gaul with us but felt she could not leave Benjamin behind, as he had been so kind to her. I assured her we would not leave her behind ever again! In fact, she would live there happily for the next five years before she died peacefully in her sleep in 86 CE aged 77 years old.

But sadly not Jean Claude. He stayed at our family home in Alexandria; he still had a business to run, and wanted to keep an eye on our house. Also, we could not live at Lake Mareotis as man and wife. Judas stayed with him to finish his apprenticeship - almost four years. They would visit the girls and I at weekends and I would stay in Alexandria from time to time; I still loved Jean Claude very much but it was a sacrifice I had signed up for before I was born.

When Jean Claude retired and Judas had finished his apprenticeship they would be able to join us permanently.. On many nights I would lie in bed awake, looking forward to that day...

CHAPTER XXI

April 82 CE: John's exile to Patmos and life in Ephesus

The Roman Emperor Domitian, younger brother of Titus, who came into power in 81 CE, was jealous of John's fame and summoned him to Rome. He thought it would provide amusement for his subjects to have John plunged into a cauldron of boiling oil outside the gate Porta Latina. A great crowd gathered, so it was much to Domitian's disappointment and horror when John came out unscathed. Seeing that this treatment had not deterred him from preaching, the emperor exiled him to the island of Patmos, where living alone, he wrote The Book of Revelation. At this time John was 81 years old.

Domitian's reign came to an end in September 96 CE when he was assassinated by court officials because he was a cruel and paranoid tyrant. He was succeeded the same day by his advisor Nerva. Domitian's memory was condemned to oblivion by the Roman Senate, revoking all his decrees.

And so at the grand age of 95 John was released and returned to Ephesus with honour, and the crowds ran out to meet him, crying,

"Blessed is he who comes in the name of the Lord!".

As he entered the city, a woman named Drusiana, who had been a dear friend of his and had looked forward more than anyone to his return, was being carried out for burial. Drusiana's family, and the widows and orphans of Ephesus, said to John,

"We were about to bury Drusiana, who, following your instructions, nourished us all with the word of our Lord in your absence. Yearning for your return she used to say; 'Ah, if only if I could see the apostle of our Lord once more before I die! And now you have returned but she was unable to see you!'

John thereupon ordered them to set down the frame, unbind the body, and said,

"Drusiana, may my Lord Jesus Christ raise you to life! Arise, go to your house and prepare food for me!"

Drusiana got up and went straight to her house as the apostle had commanded, as if she had awoken from sleep, not death.

The following day a philosopher named Crato called the people together in the public square to show them how they should despise the world. He had ordered two young brothers, very rich, to sell their property, buy the most priceless gems with the proceeds, and to smash them to bits while everyone watched. John happened to be passing and denounced this sort of contempt for the world, citing three reasons. Firstly, it wins the praise of men but is condemned by divine judgement. Secondly, such contempt cures no vices and therefore is worthless, as any medicine which does not cure a disease is worthless. Thirdly, contempt of riches is of merit only when they are given away to the poor, as our Lord said to the rich young man, "If you wish to be perfect, go and sell all you have and give to the poor".

Hearing this, Crato replied, "If your master truly is the Son of God, and it is his will that these gems should benefit the poor, then put them together again, winning glory from him as I have won applause of men."

John gathered the fragments of the gems in his hand and prayed, and the stones were restored to their former shape. At this Crato and the two brothers believed, and they sold the gems and gave the money to the poor.

This induced two other wealthy young men to sell their possessions and give the proceeds to the poor; they became followers of John and believed in Jesus Christ. But one day they saw their former slaves flaunting elegant and expensive clothes, while they had but one cloak between them, and they began to have regrets. John saw their gloomy expressions, so he had some sticks and stones brought to him from the seashore, and turned them into gold and precious stones. Then he sent the young men to show their new possessions to all the goldsmiths and jewellers, and they returned a few days later saying the experts had never seen gold so pure or gems so fine. John said to them,

"Go and buy back the lands you sold! Since you have lost the treasure of heaven, be rich for a time, only to be beggars for eternity!"

He then went on to speak against riches, giving six reasons to deter us from an inordinate desire for wealth. The first in Scripture; John told the story of the gluttonous rich man, who God rejected, and the poor man Lazarus, whom God rewarded. The second from nature; we are born naked without wealth and we die without wealth. The third is seen in creation; just as the sun, the moon and the stars, the rains and the air, are common to all and shared by all, so amongst men everything should be shared. The fourth is fortune itself; the rich man is the slave of his money - he does not possess it, it possesses him, and he becomes a slave of the devil. The fifth is care and worry; the rich worry day and night about how to get more and how to keep what they have. Sixth, and last; wealth invokes the risk of loss. In the acquisition of riches there lies a twofold evil. It often leads to swollen pride in the present life and to eternal damnation in the next. A double loss - of divine grace in the present and eternal glory in the future.

While John was giving his discourse against riches, a young man who had been married only a month was being carried out for burial. His mother, a widow, prostrated herself at the apostle's feet, begging John to revive him in the name of God, as he had done for Drusiana. The apostle, after weeping and praying for a long time, raised the dead man to life and ordered him to tell the two wealthy young men how great a penalty they had incurred and how much glory they had lost. He proceeded to speak at length about the glories of paradise and the pains of hell, and said,

"Oh wretched men, I saw your angels weeping and the demons gloating over you!". He further told them they had lost eternal palaces of shining gems, filled with banquets, abounding in delights and lasting joys. He also spoke of the eight pains of hell, which are named in the following verse,

Vermes et Tenebrae flagellum frigus et ignis

Daemonis adspectus scelerum confusion luctus

(i.e. worms, darkness, the lash, cold, fire, the sight of the devil, remorse for sins, grief)

The revived man and the two others fell at John's feet and implored him to obtain mercy for them. John replied,

"Do penance for thirty days, and during that time pray that the sticks and stones may revert to their former nature. After this time, put them back where you found them." They followed John's instructions, and the gold and jewels became sticks and stones once more. Thereupon the young men received the grace of all the virtues that had been theirs.

When John had preached throughout Asia, the idol-worshippers stirred up a riot among the people, and they dragged him to the temple of Diana and tried to force him to offer sacrifice to the goddess. John proposed an alternative: if by invoking Diana they overturned the church of Christ, he would offer sacrifice to the idols; but if by invoking Christ he destroyed Diana's temple, they would believe in Christ. The majority of the people agreed: they all left the building; as the apostle prayed, the temple collapsed to the ground and the statue of Diana was reduced to dust.

But the high priest Aristodemus incited an even greater commotion among the people, with the two parties at the point of coming to blows. John asked the priest,

"What do you want me to do to restore order?"

The high priest answered,

"If you want me to believe in your God, I will give you poison to drink. If it does not harm you, it will be clear that your master is the true God." John replied,

"I will do as you say, but first, I want to see it kill some others, to make you fear its power even more."

So Aristodemus requested permission from the high consul for the release of two criminals condemned to decapitation, and in the presence of the crowd, gave them the poison. They drank it and fell to the ground dead. The crowd mockingly sighed in unison. John took the same cup, armed himself with the sign of the cross and drained the drink. You could hear a pin drop as the crowd studied him in expectant silence, and when they were sure he had suffered no harm, cheered and rejoiced praising God.

However, Aristodemus was not ready to concede. He turned to John and said,

"If you can bring the two men back to life, I will not hesitate to believe."
John handed him his cloak.

"Why do you give me your cloak?" the priest enquired.

"To make you think twice and give up your disbelief!" John cried.

"No mantle of yours will ever make me believe!" the priest retorted.

John was unmoved and said to him,

"Go and spread this cloak over the corpses, and say, 'The Apostle of Christ
has sent me to you, that you may rise in the name of Christ.'"

The priest did as he was bidden, and the dead men arose at once. Finally
the High Priest and the High Consul believed, and John baptized them and
their families. Sometime later they would build a church in honour of Saint
John.

On one occasion when John went to take a bath in Ephesus, he saw the
heretic Cerinthus in the baths and immediately hurried out, saying,

"Let us get out for fear the bathhouse might cave in on us, because
Cerinthus, an enemy of the truth, is bathing here."

One of John's followers gave him a live partridge as it was considered a
delicacy and greatly sought after. But John gently held and stroked the bird.
Seeing this, a boy laughed and called to his companions,

"Come and watch this old man playing with a little bird like a child!"

John called the boy over, pointed at the bow in his hand and asked him
what he did with it. The boy answered excitedly,

"We shoot birds and animals!" The boy proceeded to stretch the
bowstring as far as he could; he stood there for some time but John said
nothing and so he loosened it. John asked him why he loosened the
bowstring and the boy replied,

"Because if you keep it stretched too long, it gets too weak to shoot the arrows." So John told him,

"That is how it is with human fragility; we would have less strength and focus for contemplation if we never relaxed and refused to give in occasionally to our weaknesses. So too the eagle, which flies higher than any other bird and looks straight into the sun, yet by its nature must come down again, and the human spirit, after it rests a while from contemplation, is refreshed and returns more readily to heavenly thoughts".

John stayed in Ephesus for the rest of his days. He grew so feeble he had to be supported by his disciples on his way to church. He would pause frequently, repeating over and over the same words,

"My sons, love one another!" One day, one of his followers asked him,

"Master, why are you always saying the same words?" John replied,

"Because it is the commandment of the Lord, and if this alone is obeyed, it is enough." When John was in his ninety-ninth year Christ appeared to him with his disciples,

"Come to me my beloved, the time has come for you to feast at my table with your brothers." John rose and prepared to go, but the Lord said,

"You will come to me on Sunday."

Early Sunday morning the church that had been built in his name was overflowing with his followers. At the first cockcrow he preached to them, exhorting them to be steadfast in their faith and fervent in obeying the commandments of God. Then he had a square grave dug near the altar, ensuring the earth was carried outside the church. He went down into the grave and, raising his hands to God, said,

"Lord Jesus Christ, you have invited me to your table, and behold I come! I thank you for welcoming me there and knowing that I have longed for you with all my heart."

When he had said this prayer a light shone around him, so bright the onlookers were blinded and he was hidden from sight. When the light faded away, the grave was seen to be filled with manna, so that the bottom of the grave appeared to be covered with fine sand, as you would see at the bottom of a spring.

———————————

Mother came to me one night and related the above account which I recorded word for word - just some of the many miracles and good works John performed in his lifetime. The truth had to be told, but she wanted to give a balanced account of his life. We are all imperfect as long as we exist in the human form and Mother had forgiven John many years ago.

She would never wish for him to be remembered as anything other than a faithful servant of our Lord Jesus Christ.

CHAPTER XXII

May 82 CE: Lake Mareotis

For the next two years I woke up every night between 3 and 5 am when Mother would transmit information to me. After morning prayers I would write down what she told me, as quickly as I could so I would not forget her words. But I never seemed to; they echoed in my head until they were safely delivered onto the papyrus. I wrote *Codex V: The Revelation of Paul, The First Revelation of James, The Second Revelation of James, The Revelation of Adam* and *The Gospel of Judas.*

Of all the writings Mother transmitted, *The Gospel of Judas* gave me the most pleasure. Beloved Judas was clearly vindicated and singled out by Yeshua as the most special of all. I never knew him but Mother spoke of him often with a wistful look in her eyes. In his honour and in memory of the injustice of it all I named my own son after him.

After that I never dipped my pen in ink again. My children took on the mantle, and how they shone! Mother would have been so proud of them. I certainly was!

In 84 CE Anne wrote Codex VI: *The Acts of Peter and the Twelve Apostles; The Thunder, Perfect Mind; Authoritative Discourse, The Concept of our Great Power, Excerpt from Plato's Republic, The Discourse on the Eighth and Ninth, The Prayer of Thanksgiving and Excerpt from the Perfect Discourse.*

In 86 CE Mary wrote *Codex VIII: Zostrianos and The Letter of Peter to Philip.* In 88 CE she wrote *The Sentences of Sextus* from *Codex XII.*

After finishing his apprenticeship, Judas wanted to visit the communities that had been established by his grandmother over 50 years ago and travelled for three years from 85 - 88 CE. He spent most of that time in Syria, more specifically Antioch, which he loved. In 87 CE he wrote *The Paraphrase of Shem*, the first tractate from *Codex VII.*

He also met and fell in love with a young Greek woman named Helena. He said she was blonde with blue eyes, from a respectable family and a good Christian. He wrote to me asking for my permission to marry, which I did not hesitate to give. I was acutely aware of my children carrying on Yeshua's bloodline, and it did not look like Mary and Anne were interested in marriage. It was down to Judas. In 88 CE Judas returned home with his bride, accompanied by a beautiful three month old baby boy named John Julius! My heart all but exploded when I looked at this blond, blue eyed baby, contentedly gurgling away in his mother's arms. He looked the image of her - she was beautiful, and seemed sweet and kind. I could see the attraction for Judas. Not that they could live as man and wife - I hoped that would not prove too much of a challenge for a young married couple..

Between 88 - 90 CE Judas wrote *The Second Discourse of Great Seth, The Revelation of Peter, The Teachings of Silvanus* and *The Three Steles of Seth* from *Codex VII*.

Jean Claude could not bear to miss out on his new grandson and took early retirement in 88 CE to join us all at Lake Mareotis. He sold half of his business to one of his long-standing employees, and said there would always be a trade for Judas if he ever wanted to return to 'normal' life. It was wonderful for us all to be together again, with the unexpected bonus of John Julius to fuss over!

And so life continued at Lake Mareotis. The 'children' were all in their thirties and organized the running of our community as a cooperative. Everyone was involved, happily.

I had been unwell for some months, suffering fevers day and night, when Mother came to me in July 94 CE and said I would be leaving this world in twelve months time. I was grateful to have time to prepare. There was nowhere I wanted to travel and nothing else I wished to do - I was content. I was relinquished from all active duties; when I was well enough I would spend hours reading to John Julius. I had had a happy life and was happy to be buried at the place I was born, over 60 years ago. Jean Claude was such a sweet soul and comfort to me in my final months - I was so privileged and grateful to have experienced the kind of love that lasts a lifetime... I was blessed beyond belief.

Mary, as my eldest daughter, inherited the sacred secrets I had learned at the Mystery School of Akhenaten. I dictated from my bed as my health failed. She in turn would choose her own successor when her time on earth drew to a close. I consulted Mary and Anne before I made Judas the leader of the community. He would also become the most prolific writer of all! He wrote *Codices IX, X, XI* and *XIII* between 96 - 101 CE. I made reference to him at the end of *The Secret Book of James*,

"They will become enlightened through me, by my faith, and through another's that is better than mine. I wish mine to be the lesser."

I loved all my children equally so I did not name him in person, but of course he knew who I was referring to.

Mary and Anne chose not to marry; they had been brought up listening to tales of my unconventional but happy childhood living with Mother Mary and Mother Salome, so they knew they did not have to marry and have children to achieve fullness. Besides, their hearts and souls belonged to their work at the community and it was not designed for married life.

They all became keepers of the three copies of the codices; their names and the whereabouts of the tractates would never be written down. This information would be handed down to the next generation by word of mouth only. We had, and always would have, enemies who would happily burn our writings, if not our very selves. They had been written in the name of Universal Truth and it was important they survived for the sake of humanity. Yeshua had foretold they would be buried for a long time and rediscovered when humanity was in need of the mysteries contained within them, and at a time when they were sufficiently inspired to understand them...

They would reveal themselves when the time was right, to those who had eyes to see and ears to hear...

Sarah du Bois
(nee Magdalene),
Lake Mareotis, July 95 CE

EPILOGUE

I have written these words in less than six months. Like the two central characters, Mary and Sarah, I was awoken every night between 3 and 5am and the ideas just flowed through. It has been a surreal experience and has felt like I have been living a double life during this time - in two worlds, then and now... When I look at my family and some of my close friends, I see them as characters in the book - acting out dramas, then and now. I have trusted my intuition and the process; I have been 'guided' and information came to me as it became relevant to the story in a most orderly fashion that my mere mind could never have organized!

Is this story *true* I hear you ask?

Alexandria would have been an obvious safe refuge for Mary Magdalene and her inner circle, home to the largest Jewish population outside Judea. At that time it was far more egalitarian than her homeland, making it possible for her to set up and lead a community there. Philo in his writings talks reverently about a community located by the shores of Lake Mareotis, the Alexandria *Therapeutae*. He mentions a woman priestess, but does not name her.

The Golden Legend, written in the 13th Century, relates Mary Magdalene's voyage from Alexandria to Gaul, the conversion of the governor of Gaul and his wife, and Martha's slaying of a 'dragon' or Tarasque. France has adopted Mary Magdalene, Mother Mary, Mary Salome, Sarah and Martha as their own; Saintes Maries-de-la-Mer is in the Camargue region - Mother Mary and Mary Salome are entombed in the church. Furthermore, there is an annual feast day for Sarah, who has been made the patron saint of the gypsies. The cave above la Baume forest which Mary Magdalene is repudiated to have spent twenty years or so in is looked after by an adjoining Benedictine monastery to this day.

In 1279, Charles, nephew of King Louis IX of France, reputedly discovered Mary Magdalene's remains at the church of St Maximin-la-Sainte-Baume in Provence. The King transferred the relics to the church's crypt in 1280, where they still are today. Every year the feast day of Mary Magdalene is celebrated on the 22nd July much to the delight of her followers.

The implications of this story are momentous and will *shake* the foundations of the papacy. Ironically, they will be more outraged at the suggestion that Mary Magdalene, former *sinner*, wrote the four New Testament gospels in corroboration with Mark, Luke and Matthew. But these writings have been heavily edited and bear little resemblance to the original, uncorrupted transmissions from Yeshua.

The Nag Hammadi codices which I believe Mary, her daughter and grandchildren wrote, are where the jewels in the crown lie! They are written in an unfamiliar form and are certainly not a light read, but I for one will persist as I feel a change has occurred to me since I have been reading them. I am *heartened* by the words of Meister Ekchart,

"If you don't understand this speech, don't trouble your heart over it. For as long as a person does not become this truth, he will not understand this speech. For this is a naked truth, which has come directly out of the heart of God."

In the meantime there is someone who walks the earth today and has a connection with the Divine who understands this language. For when I read the words of *The Gospel of Mary*, for example, and listen to the words of Ratu Bagus, my heart resonates with the same *feeling*. I have learned to trust this feeling as only my heart, not my mind, knows the Truth.

We should remember that the history we read in books today is what was recorded, not necessarily what happened.

Ratu is suspicious of the written word and does not write down his teachings. Everything around us is changing, moment to moment, and once words are fixed on paper they can be misunderstood or become outdated. I have been changing my text almost daily, as ideas come through in the night from my unconscious, or beyond, unfettered by my controlling mind.

For instance, the words *'time of the End'* from the Book of Daniel are often interpreted as an apocalyptic prediction of the end of the world;

"But thou, O Daniel, shut up the words and seal the book until the time of the End." Book of Daniel, Old Testament 12:4

I am not alone in understanding this in another way, not least because I am an optimist and also we are still in existence.

Scholars believe The Book of Daniel was written in the second century BCE. The Mayans predicted 2,000 years ago that on 21st December 2012 we would start our transition from the Age of Pisces into the Age of Aquarius. This change occurs roughly every 2,150 years. So if the prediction about the *'time of the End'* was made mid second century BC, that is 150 BC, the End would be around now, and refers to the End of the Age of Pisces and not the end of the world. A time of change...

The Age of Aquarius is associated with computers, democracy, freedom, humanitarianism, idealism and philanthropy. The transition is causing great turmoil as everything with Piscean values is being exposed or unravelling; governments, corporations, individuals and even personal relationships.

We are being asked to make a choice; to cling to the old values or adopt the new evolving ones. We are moving into a 'great window of opportunity for spiritual growth'. We have an *opportunity* to become spiritual beings having a human existence, rather than human beings having a worldly experience.

Ratu Bagus has one book; when you open the cover, all that lies inside is a mirror. He is trying to tell us the answers are inside each and every one of us, we just have to look...

I have just returned from Bali - I went to seek Ratu's blessing and permission to publish my book. He has not read it - apparently he does not need to. During my two week stay I wrote or edited every night after dinner. The next day Ratu would quote lines and cite scenes from what I had written the night before! His opinion is what matters to me - so if he sees it as the *Truth* then I will close my ears to critics who will try to dismiss me as a modern day heretic or fantasist.

I will let the Universal Truth speak for itself.

For now is the time...

March 2019

LIST OF CHARACTERS

MARY MAGDALENE Born in Magdala in 7 CE. Moved to Alexandria, Egypt and founded Lake Mareotis community in 33 CE. Fled to Marseilles, Gaul in 43 CE and moved to La Baume grotto in 46 CE. She died in France in 63 CE aged 57.

MARY, MOTHER OF JESUS Born in 15 BCE. Accompanied Mary Magdalene on her travels and died in St Maries-de-la-Mer in 57 CE aged 72. Half- sister of Mary Salome.

MARY SALOME Born in 13 BCE Half-sister of Mary Mother of Jesus and full sister of Joseph of Arimathea. Accompanied Mary Magdalene on her travels and lived in St Maries-de-la-Mer until her death in 56 CE aged 69.

JOSEPH OF ARIMATHEA Born in Marmorica, Egypt in 17 BCE. Half brother of Mary Salome. Wealthy tin merchant who sailed as far as South America. Took Mary Magdalene out of Jerusalem in 33 CE and also to Gaul in 43 CE. Retired to a monastery in Compostela, Spain in 57 CE where he lived until his death in 59 CE aged 76.

LAZARUS OF BETHANY Born in Magdala in 4 CE. Elder brother to Mary Magdalene and Martha. Accompanied Mary Magdalene to Alexandria and Gaul. Became first Bishop of Marseilles and was beheaded in 61 CE.

MARTHA Born in 9 CE, younger sister of Mary Magdalene and Lazarus. Accompanied Mary Magdalene to Alexandria and France. Moved to St Maries-de-la-Mer in 46 CE and then to Tarscon in 48 CE where she lived until her death in 67 CE aged 58. Had a maid called MARTILLA who travelled from Bethany with Martha and remained in service to her for the rest of her life.

MAXIMIN Born in 18 BCE. Accompanied Mary Magdalene from Bethany to Alexandria and to Gaul. Became Bishop of Aix en Provence and died in 63 CE aged 81. Buried next to Mary Magdalene.

SARAH Daughter of Mary Magdalene and Yeshua born in Alexandria in September 33 CE. Sailed to Marseilles, Gaul in 43 CE with Mary Magdalene and family. Lived in St Maries-de-la-Mer with the two Marys. Married Jean Claude du Bois, a cabinet maker in 56 CE in St Maries-de-la-Mer. They had three children: Mary born in 58 CE, Anne born in 59 CE and Judas born in 63 CE - all born in Gaul. Moved to Alexandria after death of Mary Magdalene in 63 CE. She died at Lake Mareotis in 95 CE.

THE 12 APOSTLES

1 **Judas Iscariot** - stoned to death in Jerusalem
2 **Simon Peter**, fisherman, brother of Andrew - crucified by Nero in Rome
3 **Andrew**, fisherman, brother of Simon Peter - crucified in Achaia, Greece
4 **James**, son of Alpheus - stoned to death in Jerusalem
5 **James**, son of Zebedee, became 1st Bishop of Jerusalem - stoned to death
6 **John**, son of Zebedee, brother of James - died of old age in Ephesus
7 **Matthew/Levi** - died of old age in Parthia (Iran)
8 **Philip** - crucified upside down in Hierapolis, Turkey
9 **Thaddaeus/Judas** - died of old age in Turkey
10 **Simon the Zealot** - became Bishop of Jerusalem after James, died of old age
11 **Bartholomew** - crucified upside down in Armenia (Georgia)
12 **Thomas** - martyred in India
13 **Matthias** (replaced Judas) - died of old age in Jerusalem

In addition, there were 72 disciples who became followers of Yeshua, of which nine were women.

LIST OF ROMAN EMPERORS

27 BCE - 14 CE	Augustus	Died of natural causes
14 - 37 CE	Tiberius	Assassinated by Caligula?
37 - 41 CE	Caligula	Assassinated
41 - 54 CE	Claudius	Poisoned by his wife Agrippina ?
54 - 68 CE	Nero	Committed suicide
68 - 69 CE	Galba	Murdered by Praetorian Guard
69 CE	Vitellius	Murdered by Vespasian's troops
69 - 79CE	Vespasian	Died of natural causes
79 - 81 CE	Titus (son of Vespasian)	Died from fever
81 - 96 CE	Domitian (" " ")	Assassinated by court officials

LIST OF GOVERNORS OF ROMAN EGYPT

During the Roman Empire, the Governor of Roman Egypt was a Prefect who administered the Roman province of Egypt with the authority of the Emperor. The Prefect usually held office for three or four years: any knowledge of Egypt and its complex traditions of religion and politics was incidental - his record of Roman service and how much he was in favour with the emperor were more important.

33 - 38 CE	Aulus Avilius Flaccus
38 - 41 CE	Gaius Vitrasius Pollio
41 - 42 CE	Lucius Aemilius Rectus
42 - 45 CE	Marcus Heius
45 - 48 CE	Gaius Julius Postumus
48 - 52 CE	Gnaeus Vergilius Capito
circa 54 CE	Lucius Lusius Geta
55 - 59 CE	Tiberius Claudius Balbillus Modestus
60 - 62 CE	Lucius Julius Vestinus
63 - 65 CE	Gaius Caecina Tuscus
66 - 69 CE	Tiberius Julius Alexander
70 CE	Lucius Peducius Colonus

Also by Julie de Vere Hunt

APOSTLE TO MARY MAGDALENE

What can Mary Magdalene teach us today?

Julie de Vere Hunt's thought-provoking appraisal of the legend of Mary Magdalene - the repentant sinner, 'bride' of Jesus, mother, teacher, healer and priestess. With an overview of what we know about Mary Magdalene from religious scholars and the Gnostic Gospels, Julie de Vere Hunt offers her personal conclusions about the myths and legends surrounding Mary Magdalene.

ISBN: 978 1 78281 461 0